Ortografía correcta
del inglés

Escuela de Idiomas De Vecchi

ORTOGRAFÍA CORRECTA DEL INGLÉS

dve
PUBLISHING

De Vecchi Ediciones participa en la plataforma digital **zonaebooks.com**
Desde su página web (www.zonaebooks.com) podrá descargarse todas las obras de nuestro catálogo disponibles en este formato.

Índice

Introducción

El lenguaje es la base de todo conocimiento. En todos los pueblos y culturas, el hombre ha incorporado, en un momento dado de su evolución, un sistema coherente de signos más o menos complejos que le ha permitido comunicarse con sus semejantes.

En un primer momento, el hombre pudo conceder un nombre a los seres y a los objetos que le rodeaban mediante el lenguaje. Más adelante, el hecho de conocer el nombre de las cosas le permitió intercambiar informaciones acerca de ellas, lo que le sirvió para desarrollar un *pensamiento abstracto*. El saber adquirido pudo fijarse, perpetuarse y enriquecerse hasta el infinito, lo que dio paso a la elaboración de las ciencias, las técnicas, las artes… o, para resumirlo en una única palabra, la *civilización*.

En la actualidad, basta con mirar alrededor para ser conscientes de la preponderancia de la escritura en la civilización occidental. Ni la aparición de la tecnología audiovisual ni la llegada de la informática han cambiado las cosas. De hecho, los faxes, los módems, las impresoras, los procesadores de textos y el *software* de reconocimiento vocal han perfeccionado la venerable pluma estilográfica y han confirmado la supremacía de la escritura.

En esta época de comunicación resulta fundamental poseer un conocimiento perfecto de la escritura de diversas lenguas, entre ellas el inglés, para transmitir informaciones de la forma más clara y precisa posible (redactar un informe, escribir una carta administrativa, etc.).

En inglés no hay muchas reglas generales de ortografía, así que lograr escribir correctamente en esta lengua resulta algo más complicado que en otras que tienen una normativa más exhaustiva, como es el caso del español. Sin embargo, sí hay algunos aspectos que están reglamentados y que inciden directamente en la correcta escritura de la lengua, como por ejemplo la pronunciación, la formación de las palabras, la puntuación y algunas cuestiones gramaticales que es necesario conocer y tener en cuenta para no cometer errores importantes. En este libro se explican de forma clara y sencilla todos estos aspectos, y se facilita un anexo de ejercicios con sus soluciones, porque no cabe duda de que la práctica es aquí más importante que en ningún otro caso.

EL EDITOR

Grafías y sonidos

El alfabeto inglés consta de veintiséis letras que indicaremos a continuación, junto con su correspondiente sonido figurado.

a	b	c	d	e	f	g	h	i
[ei]	[bii]	[sii]	[dii]	[ii]	[ef]	[yi]	[eitch]	[ai]

j	k	l	m	n	o	p	q	r
[yiei]	[kei]	[el]	[em]	[en]	[ou]	[pi]	[kiuu]	[a:]

s	t	u	v	w	x	y	z
[es]	[tii]	[iuu]	[vii]	[dab(l)iuu]	[eks]	[uai]	[sed]

Las vocales

Las vocales inglesas no siempre tienen el mismo sonido, y puede decirse que únicamente mantienen el sonido alfabético en tres casos:

— cuando se encuentran al final de una sílaba acentuada;

— a principio de palabra, cuando constituyen una sílaba por sí mismas;

— cuando les sigue una consonante que, a su vez, está seguida de una e.

Sonido de las principales vocales dobles y de los diptongos

ee Se lee *ii* (*i* larga).

oo Se lee *u* o bien *uu*.

ais/ay Se leen *ei*.

ea Se puede leer *ii*, *e*, *eu*.

ei Se lee *ei*.

ey Se lee *ei*, *i*.

ew Se lee *iu* (*u*, si le precede una *r*).

oa, oe Se leen *ou*.

ow Se lee *au*, *ou*.

ou Se lee *au*, *a*, *u*.

Las consonantes

Las consonantes se pronuncian normalmente.

No obstante, veamos a continuación algunas distinciones de sonido:

k Deberá leerse siempre como la *c* española ante *a*, *o*, *u* (*casa*, *cuna*).

ch Deberá leerse siempre *ch*, como en español *mucho*.

s Deberá leerse siempre como la *s* inicial española (*sal*).

z Deberá leerse siempre como la *s* sonora española (*desde*).

j No tiene equivalencia en español. Se leerá como suena en la palabra francesa *bijou*.

h Indica siempre una aspiración al comienzo de palabra.

g/gh En medio o al comienzo de palabra, se leen generalmente como la *g* inicial española delante de *a, o, u*, o como la *j* de la palabra francesa *bijou*. Al final de palabra, la *g* se lee como la *j* francesa y el sonido *gh* equivale al español *gu* delante de las vocales *e, i*.

n Se lee *n* nasal como en el español *fango* pero pronunciado sin la *o* final.

d/t Se pronuncian casi siempre apoyando la lengua contra el paladar.

t Tiene dos sonidos distintos que equivalen aproximadamente a la *z* española de *pozo* y a la *d* de *gordo*. El segundo de estos sonidos es sonoro y se pronuncia apoyando la lengua con fuerza contra los dientes.

Otras particularidades

sc Se pronuncia *s* delante de *e, i, y*.

sh Tiene un sonido equivalente al de la *ch* francesa en *chapeau*.

ska/-e/-i/-o/-u Se leen con la *c* fuerte, como en la palabra francesa *scandal*.

ph Se pronuncia *f*.

k No se lee delante de *n*.

w No se lee delante de *r*.

El acento suele caer siempre sobre la primera parte de la palabra.

Las palabras

Formación del plural

Sustantivos

La gran mayoría de los nombres de cosas o animales forman el plural añadiendo una -s.

Singular	Plural	Singular	Plural
chair	chairs	book	books
silla	sillas	libro	libros
boat	boats		
barco	barcos		

El plural de los nombres que terminan con -s, -ss, -sh, -ch y -x se forma añadiendo -es.

Singular	Plural	Singular	Plural
dress	dresses	brush	brushes
vestido	vestidos	cepillo	cepillos
church	churches	box	boxes
iglesia	iglesias	caja	cajas

En los nombres que terminan en consonante seguida de -y se suprime la -y y se añade -ies, pero si el nombre termina en vocal más -y se añade sólo la -s.

Singular	Plural	Singular	Plural
lady	ladies	city	cities
dama	damas	ciudad	ciudades
boy	boys	day	days
chico	chicos	día	días

El plural de los nombres que terminan en -f y -fe se forma cambiando la f a v y añadiendo -es.

Singular	Plural	Singular	Plural
wife	wives	knife	knives
esposa	esposas	cuchillo	cuchillos
thief	thieves		
ladrón	ladrones		

El plural de los nombres que terminan en -o, precedidos por una vocal, se forma añadiendo una -s. A los nombres que terminan en -o, precedidos de una consonante, se les añade -es para formar el plural.

Singular	Plural	Singular	Plural
radio	radios	hero	heroes
radio	radios	héroe	héroes
potato	potatoes		
patata	patatas		

El plural de los nombres que terminan en -o y se refieren a la música, vayan acompañados de vocal o consonante, se forma añadiendo una -s.

Singular	Plural	Singular	Plural
piano	*pianos*	*soprano*	*sopranos*
piano	pianos	soprano	sopranos

Hay nombres que tienen formas irregulares en plural. Son los que no emplean la -s, sino que cambian de forma. Los más frecuentes son los siguientes:

Singular	Plural	Singular	Plural
man	*men*	*woman*	*women*
hombre	hombres	mujer	mujeres
child	*children*	*tooth*	*teeth*
niño/-a	niños/-as	diente	dientes
foot	*feet*	*mouse*	*mice*
pie	pies	ratón	ratones
ox	*oxen*	*goose*	*geese*
buey	bueyes	oca	ocas
goose	*geese*		
ganso	gansos		

El plural de los nombres compuestos se forma poniendo en este número el nombre modificador.

Singular	Plural	Singular	Plural
mother-in-law	*mothers-in-law*	*passer-by*	*passers-by*
suegra	suegras	transeúnte	transeúntes

El plural de nombres extranjeros:

Singular	Plural	Singular	Plural
datum	*data*	*analysis*	*analyses*
dato	datos	análisis	análisis
bacillus	*bacilli*	*radio*	*radii*
bacilo	bacilos	radio	radios

El plural de los números y de las letras se forma añadiendo un apóstrofo y una -s.

Ej.: There are two s's in necessary.
Hay dos eses en *necessary.*.

There are five 5's in this page.
Hay cinco cincos en esta página.

Algunos nombres son iguales en singular y en plural:

Ej.: sheep	oveja / ovejas
deer	ciervo / ciervos
species	especie / especies
Chinese	chino / chinos

Adjetivos

El adjetivo es una palabra que modifica un nombre o un pronombre, es decir, puede describir una persona o una cosa, dependiendo del caso.
Se coloca siempre antes del nombre y después del verbo *to be.*
Los adjetivos ingleses son invariables en todos los casos: por tanto, no existen formas masculinas o femeninas ni singular o plural.

Ej.: This is a nice boy.
Este es un chico simpático.

That is a nice girl.
Esta es una chica simpática.

Sujeto	Verbo	Complemento		
		(art.	*adj.*	*nombre)*
This	*is*	*a*	*large*	*television.*

Este es un televisor grande.

Ej.: old   viejo
    new   nuevo
    small   pequeño
    brown   marrón

Cuando hay más de un adjetivo se anteponen todos al nombre.

Sujeto	Verbo	Complemento			
		(art.	*adj.*	*adj.*	*nombre)*
This	*is*	*a*	*big*	*blue*	*bicycle.*

Esta es una bicicleta azul grande.

Ej.: This is a modern calculator and that is an old refrigerator.
Esta es una calculadora moderna y aquel es un refrigerador antiguo.

LOS SUSTANTIVOS COMO ADJETIVOS

Cuando el sustantivo se emplea como adjetivo, adopta todas las características de este; es decir, tampoco tiene plural.

Ej.: opera singer   *opera singers*
    cantante de ópera   cantantes de ópera
    ballet dancer   *ballet dancers*
    bailarina de ballet   bailarinas de ballet

tennis player	*tennis players*
jugador de tenis	jugadores de tenis
horror film	*horror films*
película de terror	películas de terror

Unos ejemplos interesantes:

a horse race	*a race horse*
una carrera de caballos	un caballo de carreras
a beer glass	*a glass of beer*
un vaso (vacío) o para cerveza	un vaso de cerveza (con cerveza)
a tea cup	*a cup of tea*
una taza (vacía) o para té	una taza de té (llena de té)

Derivación mediante sufijos

Para expresar que una cosa o una persona está dotado de algo, se utiliza el sufijo *-ful*.

Ej.: use (uso)	*useful* (útil)
hope (esperanza)	*hopeful* (esperanzado)
care (cuidado)	*careful* (cuidadoso)
success (éxito)	*succesful* (exitoso)

No se debe confundir este *-ful* con otro que tiene el sentido de «lleno de»:

Ej.: hand (mano)	*handful* (puñado)
spoon (cuchara)	*spoonful* (cucharada)

Para expresar que una cosa o una persona está privado de algo, se utiliza el sufijo -less.

> *Ej.: use* (uso) *useless* (inútil)
> *hope* (esperanza) *hopeless* (desesperado)

El sufijo -able corresponde al castellano -ible y -able.

> *Ej.: move* (mover) *movable* (movible)
> *comfort* (comodidad) *comfortable* (confortable, cómodo)

El sufijo castellano -ible es igual en inglés, pero tiene como prefijo una palabra latina.

> *Ej.: believe* (creer) *credible* (creíble)
> *read* (leer) *legible* (legible)

El sufijo -ist corresponde al castellano -ista.

> *Ej.: violin* (violín) *violinist* (violinista)
> *novel* (novela) *novelist* (novelista)

El sufijo -an corresponde al castellano -ano/-ana.

> *Ej.: Peru* *Peruvian* (peruano/-a)
> *America* *American* (americano/-a)

Derivación mediante prefijos

Hay algunos prefijos que se utilizan para dar un sentido negativo: *dis-*, *un-*, *in-*, *im-*, *mis-*.

Ej.: appear (aparecer)	*disappear* (desaparecer)
happy (feliz)	*unhappy* (infeliz, desgraciado)
direct (directo)	*indirect* (indirecto)
possible (posible)	*impossible* (imposible)
understand (entender)	*misunderstand* (entender mal)

Para expresar exceso o superioridad se utiliza el prefijo *over-*.

Ej.: sleep (dormir)	*oversleep* (dormir demasiado)
take (coger)	*overtake* (sobrepasar)

Para expresar inferioridad se utiliza el prefijo *under-*.

Ej.: go (ir)	*undergo* (sufrir)
value (valor)	*undervalue* (despreciar)
sell (vender)	*undersell* (vender a bajo precio)

Para expresar acciones ejercidas por uno mismo, con autonomía, se utiliza el prefijo *self-*.

Ej.: self-control (autodominio)
self-government (autogobierno)
self-taught man (autodidacta)

Los signos de puntuación

Los signos de puntuación se emplean en inglés de una manera muy similar a como se utilizan en español, con algunas excepciones que se comentarán oportunamente.

Punto

a) Se coloca al final de la frase, a menos que esta tenga carácter interrogativo o exclamativo.

Ej.: *Look at those children.* *They're going to hurt*
 Mira a aquellos niños. *themselves.*
  Se van a hacer daño.

b) Se utiliza en las abreviaturas:

Ej.: *Mr., Dr., Lincoln Ave., Elm St.*
 Señor, doctor, av. Lincoln, calle Elm

Coma

a) Se emplea para indicar una pausa dentro de una frase.

Ej.: By the way, she's the wife of the owner of that restaurant.
A propósito, es la esposa del dueño de aquel restaurante.

b) Como nexo de unión en series de palabras o frases.

Ej.: I would like to see blouses, belts and skirts.
Me gustaría ver blusas, cinturones y faldas.

c) Para separar del resto de la oración el nombre de la persona a quien se dirige la palabra (vocativo).

Ej.: Come this way, madam.
Por aquí, señora.

d) Para separar una conversación que se cita.

Ej.: He said, «I'll help you.»
Él dijo: «Te voy a ayudar».

Punto y coma

Se utiliza para separar dos partes bien diferenciadas en el interior de una misma frase.

Ej.: She wants to leave on the night train; I did not.
Ella quiere marcharse con el tren de la noche; yo, no.

Dos puntos

a) Se emplean al enunciar una lista e incluir a continuación los miembros que la componen.

Ej.: The four seasons are: spring, summer, autumn, winter.
Las cuatro estaciones son: primavera, verano, otoño, invierno.

b) En la correspondencia, después del saludo:

Ej.: Dear Mr. Jones:
Querido Sr. Jones:

Puntos suspensivos

Se utilizan para señalar la omisión de una o más palabras en la construcción normal de la frase.

Ej.: Alice, whose sister you know...
Alicia, cuya hermana conoces...

Ej.: She wrote in her diary: «... and my sister always gets everything she wishes».
Ella escribió en su diario: «... y mi hermana siempre consigue lo que quiere».

Interrogación

Se escribe al final de las frases interrogativas directas.

Ej.: What is the matter with you?
¿Qué te pasa?

Exclamación o admiración

a) Se incluye al final de las frases que expresan emociones.

Ej.: I did it myself!
   ¡Lo hice yo mismo!

b) También se usa en interjecciones u onomatopeyas.

Ej.: Waiter!
   ¡Camarero!

   Bang, bang!
   ¡Pum, pum!

Guión

a) Se emplea en las palabras compuestas.

| *Ej.: father-in-law* | *forty-two* | *self-service* |
| suegro | cuarenta y dos | autoservicio |

b) Para unir algunos prefijos a palabras.

| *Ej.: anti-aircraft* | *pre-established* |
| antiaéreo | preestablecido |

c) Para separar palabras al final de la línea.

Raya o guión largo

a) Se emplea para marcar un inciso en el interior de una frase.

Ej.: The surplus population —as many as 35 million— was driven eastwards.

La población excedente —unos 35 millones— fue conducida hacia el este.

b) Puede utilizarse para separar una oración de las palabras o expresiones que la explican.

En español este uso es incorrecto y se sustituye por los dos puntos.

Ej.: Rembrandt's work can be divided into three categories —portraits, landscapes and history paintings.
La obra de Rembrandt se puede dividir en tres categorías: retratos, paisajes y pintura histórica.

Paréntesis

Se emplea para resaltar o separar algún concepto en el interior de una frase.

Ej.: My cousins (Sam and Daisy) learn spanish.
Mis primos (Sam y Daisy) aprenden español.

Apóstrofo

a) Se utiliza para señalar la omisión de una o más letras en las contracciones:

I am	I'm
you are	you're
it is	it's
do not	don't
it is not	it isn't

b) Para escribir el genitivo sajón.

Ej.: The cat's leg.
La pata del gato.

c) Cuando el sustantivo termina en -s, el genitivo se expresa sólo con el apóstrofo.

Ej.: The mechanics' uniforms are blue.
Los uniformes de los mecánicos son azules.

Comillas

a) Se emplean para acotar las palabras o pensamientos expresados en los diálogos. En español se utiliza, en cambio, el guión largo para señalar el inicio y los intercalados aclaratorios.

Ej.: «Engagement!» cried Marianne. «There has been no engagement».
—¡Compromiso! —gritó Marianne—. No ha habido ningún compromiso.

b) Para escribir los títulos de libros, películas, etc., aunque resulta preferible el uso de la letra cursiva.

Ej.: Bram Stoker wrote «Dracula».
Bram Stoker escribió «Drácula».

c) Para destacar una palabra o frase, aunque es más recomendable el empleo de la letra cursiva.

Ej.: The word «holiday» has three vowels.
La palabra «holiday» tiene tres vocales.

Ortografía gramatical

El artículo

a) Determinado: los artículos determinados españoles (*el, la, los, las*) tienen un solo equivalente en inglés: *the,* que se utiliza tanto para el femenino como para el masculino, así como para el singular y el plural.

Singular	Plural	Singular	Plural
the girl	the girls	the boy	the boys
la chica	las chicas	el chico	los chicos
the cat	the cats		
el gato	los gatos		

Se pronuncia *the* delante de consonante y *thi* delante de vocal.

b) Indeterminado: los singulares *un* y *una* equivalen en inglés a la palabra *a.* Delante de una palabra que comienza con vocal, en lugar de *a* se emplea *an* para facilitar la pronunciación. Sucede lo mismo cuando la palabra comienza con *h* muda, por ejemplo: *hour* (hora), *heir* (heredero), *honest* (honesto), *honour* (honor).

Ej.: a car   *a boy*
   un coche   un chico
   an apple   *an orange*
   una manzana   una naranja

Los plurales *unos* y *unas* equivalen a *some*.

Ej.: some girls   *some boys*
   unas chicas   unos chicos

El artículo indeterminado *a* se pronuncia como una e muy retrasada y se une a la palabra siguiente.

El genitivo sajón

El genitivo sajón ('s) se usa generalmente con el complemento de posesión:

Ej.: my brother's suit
   el traje de mi hermano

Hay que tener en cuenta que se usa sobre todo con los nombres de personas, de animales y de conceptos personificados.

Ej.: the boy's socks   los calcetines del niño
   the horse's legs   las patas del caballo
   England's cities   las ciudades de Inglaterra

No se usa nunca con los nombres de las cosas, pero puede emplearse idiomáticamente en alguna expresión de tiempo o distancia.

Ej.: today's news   las noticias de hoy
    last year's results   los resultados del año pasado
    a mile's walk   un paseo de una milla

Se utiliza frecuentemente para indicar iglesias, negocios, viviendas, etc., sobreentendiendo tales nombres.

Ej.: I went to Saint Peter's.   Fui a San Pedro.
    (se sobreentiende *church*, iglesia)

    He lives at his brother's.   Vive con su hermano.
    (se sobreentiende *house*, casa)

La *s* del genitivo sajón presenta diversas peculiaridades:

— Cuando el nombre del poseedor es un plural terminado en -s, se añade sólo el apóstrofo.

    Ej.: the girls' stockings
    las medias de las chicas

— Cuando el nombre del poseedor está compuesto de varias palabras, el apóstrofo y la *s* se ponen sólo al final de la última.

    Ej.: the queen of England's castles
    los castillos de la reina de Inglaterra

— Si los poseedores son dos, hay varias opciones.

    Ej.: John and Mary's house   la casa de Juan y María
    (propiedad común: la casa pertenece a ambos)

John's and Mary's books
los libros de Juan y de María
(propiedad separada: parte de los libros pertenece
a Juan y el resto a María)

No debe confundirse 's con la forma contracta de las formas verbales *is* o *has*.

Ej.: Mary's in school.
(Mary is in school.)   María está en la escuela.

Mary's got a cat.
(Mary has got a cat.)   María tiene un gato.

This is Mary's purse.   Esta es la bolsa de María.

El genitivo también se forma con la preposición *of (the)* que se utiliza para los poseedores inanimados. Se emplea con el complemento de especificación.

Ej.: the doors of the car   las puertas del coche

También se usa con el complemento de materia.

Ej.: a dress of silk   un vestido de seda

Sin embargo, en este caso, es más común recurrir a la forma de los nombres compuestos: *a silk dress*.

There is, there are

Ej.: There is a red car on the corner.
Hay un coche rojo en la esquina.

There are expensive clocks in this shop.
Hay relojes caros en esta tienda.

Aunque la palabra *there* significa «allí», en combinación con *is* o *are* pierde este sentido y se convierte en «hay». En inglés se utiliza uno u otro según se trate de singular o de plural, a diferencia del castellano, en que *hay* es invariable.

Formas interrogativa y negativa

Ej.: *Is there a dryer in the kitchen?*
¿Hay una secadora en la cocina?

No, there isn't a dryer in the kitchen.
No, no hay una secadora en la cocina.

Are there two records on the table?
¿Hay dos discos sobre la mesa?

No, there aren't two records on the table.
No, no hay dos discos sobre la mesa.

Respuestas cortas

Ej.: *Is there a magazine on the bed?*
¿Hay una revista encima de la cama?
Yes, there is.
Sí, la hay.
No, there isn't.
No, no la hay.

Are there two cassettes in the dining room?
¿Hay dos cintas en el comedor?
Yes, there are.
Sí, las hay.
No, there aren't.
No, no las hay.

Are there any cars in the street?
¿Hay algunos coches en la calle?
Yes, there are some.
Sí, hay algunos.
No, there aren't any.
No, no hay ninguno.

En los plurales *there are, are there?, there aren't,* normalmente se emplean las palabras *some* o *any* (unos, algunos). *Some* se usa en las frases afirmativas, y *any*, en las negativas.

Los grados de comparación

Comparativo de igualdad

En las oraciones afirmativas este comparativo se forma con *as... as...,* que equivale a «tan... como...». En las oraciones negativas e interrogativas el primer *as* pasa a ser *not as...*

Comparativo de superioridad

Se forma añadiendo la terminación *-er* a los adjetivos y a los adverbios monosílabos o bisílabos que terminan en

-er, -le, -li, -y, -o, -or y *-ow*. El segundo término de la comparación se introduce con *than*.

Si el adjetivo termina en *-y*, esta pasa a *i* antes de añadir la terminación *-er*.

Los adjetivos de dos o más sílabas y los adverbios terminados en *-ly* forman el comparativo de superioridad anteponiendo la partícula *more*.

Comparativo de inferioridad

Se forma anteponiendo la partícula *less* al adjetivo. El segundo término de la comparación se introduce con *than*.

Superlativo relativo de superioridad

Se forma añadiendo la terminación *-est* a los adjetivos monosílabos o bisílabos que terminan en *-er, -le, -li, -y, -o, -or* o *-ow* y precediéndolos con el artículo *the*. Sin embargo, si se trata más bien de una comparación entre dos personas o cosas, se emplea la forma del comparativo de superioridad con *-er*, siempre precedido del artículo *the*.

Si el adjetivo termina en *-y*, esta cambia a *i* antes de añadir la terminación *-est*.

Los adjetivos monosílabos terminados en consonante precedida de una sola vocal doblan la consonante antes de añadir *-est*.

Los adjetivos de dos o más sílabas y los adverbios terminados en *-ly* forman el superlativo relativo de superioridad anteponiendo al adjetivo *the most*.

El complemento no se introduce con *than* (puesto que no se trata del segundo término de la comparación), sino con *in* y, más raramente, con *of*.

Superlativo relativo de inferioridad

Se forma colocando delante del adjetivo *the least*. El complemento no se introduce con la partícula *than* (puesto que no se trata del segundo término de la comparación), sino con *in* y, más raramente, con *of*.

Superlativo absoluto

Se forma anteponiendo *very* al adjetivo.

Comparativos y superlativos irregulares

Los adjetivos comparativos y superlativos irregulares más habituales son:

Adjetivo	Comparativo	Superlativo
good	better	best
bad	worse	worst
far	farther / further	farthest / furthest
old	older / elder	oldest / eldest
little	less	least
a lot of	more	most

Pronombres

Pronombres personales

Se agrupan en dos categorías: pronombres personales con función de sujeto *(I, you, he / she / it, we, you, they)* y pronombres personales que tienen función de objeto *(me, you, him / her / it, us, you, them)*.

En inglés, los pronombres personales con función de sujeto nunca deben omitirse en la oración.

Se usa la forma de objeto cuando el pronombre es complemento directo o indirecto, después de una preposición y después del verbo *to be* en el predicado nominal.

Pronombres demostrativos

En inglés existen dos tipos de pronombres demostrativos, atendiendo a su función:

— *this, that, these* y *those* son invariables en género, pero no en número. Nunca van seguidos de un sustantivo y sirven para indicar proximidad *(this, these)* o lejanía *(that, those)* en el tiempo y en el espacio, desde el punto de vista de quien habla;
— *one* se emplea para evitar repetir un sustantivo en singular, y *ones,* cuando es plural. Se usan detrás de: un adjetivo calificativo, *the, every, each,* un adjetivo demostrativo o *which*.

Pronombres indefinidos

Pueden ser simples *(some, any)* o compuestos *(someone, somebody, anyone, no one, none, nobody, everyone, everybody, something, anything, nothing, everything)*. *Some* y sus compuestos se usan en oraciones afirmativas e interrogativas, además de en los ofrecimientos. *Any* y sus compuestos, en cambio, se emplean en las oraciones negativas y en las interrogativas negativas. *Nobody, nothing, no one* y *none* expresan una negación y, por tanto, no deben ir acompañados de otras negaciones.

OTROS PRONOMBRES INDEFINIDOS Y CUANTITATIVOS

Little: siempre en singular; significa «poco».

A little: siempre en singular; significa «un poco».

Few: plural; significa «pocos».

A few: plural; significa «algunos, unos cuantos».

Much: cuantitativo, sólo precede a sustantivos en singular; significa «mucho».

Many: cuantitativo, únicamente precede a sustantivos en plural; significa «muchos».

A lot (of): utilizado en lugar de *much* o *many* en las oraciones afirmativas.

Either... or...: se usa con el significado de «o... o...».

Neither: equivale a «ni el uno ni el otro, ninguno de los dos».

Neither... nor...: se usa con el significado de «ni... ni...».

Each, every: significan «cada, todos, cada uno/a».

Both: invariable; significa «ambos, los dos».

All: usado con el significado de «todo, todos» es siempre invariable; cuando va seguido de un sustantivo singular significa «cada».

Several: significa «vario/a/s».

Such: significa «tal, tales, tan, tanto»; es invariable y nunca va precedido de artículo; cuando acompaña a un sustantivo singular, va seguido del artículo indeterminado.

Plenty of...: equivale a «mucho, mucha, muchos, muchas».

Enough: significa «bastante»; puede preceder o ir detrás del sustantivo.

Certain: significa «cierto/a, ciertos/as, alguien» en el sentido de «cierta persona / cosa»; cuando acompaña a un sustantivo singular, debe ir precedido del artículo indeterminado; si acompaña a un sustantivo plural, va solo.

Pronombres posesivos

Los pronombres posesivos en inglés son *mine, yours, his, her, its, ours* y *theirs*; son invariables y nunca van precedidos de artículo.

Pronombres reflexivos

Los pronombres reflexivos en inglés son *myself, yourself, himself, herself, itself, ourselves, yourselves* y *themselves*. Se usan cuando el sujeto y el complemento indirecto coinciden, aunque también pueden servir para enfatizar un sustantivo o un pronombre.

Pronombres recíprocos

Son *each other* y *one another*. *Each other* se emplea cuando la acción se realiza entre dos personas; *one another*, en cambio, cuando la acción se realiza entre más de dos personas o un número indeterminado de ellas.

Pronombres relativos

Las oraciones de relativo van introducidas en inglés por uno de los siguientes pronombres relativos:

Who: se usa sólo para las personas; puede tener función de sujeto o de complemento.

Which: se usa para cosas; puede tener función de sujeto o de complemento, y puede referirse a toda una oración.

Whom: se usa para las personas, en lugar de *who*, cuando es complemento indirecto de la oración de relativo o hay una preposición.

En lugar de un pronombre relativo seguido de un verbo en forma activa, también se forman oraciones de relativo con el verbo acabado en *-ing*.

En lugar de un pronombre relativo seguido de un verbo en forma pasiva, también se pueden formar oraciones de relativo con el participio pasado.

El pronombre relativo también se puede sustituir por un infinitivo.

Adjetivos

Adjetivos demostrativos

Al igual que los pronombres, los adjetivos *this, that, these* y *those* son invariables en género, pero no en número. Se emplean para indicar proximidad (*this, these*) o lejanía (*that, those*), en el tiempo y en el espacio, desde el punto de vista de quien habla.

Adjetivos indefinidos

Son *some, any* y *no*, y se emplean para referirse a personas y cosas indeterminadas. En castellano se corresponden, respectivamente, con «algún, alguno, ninguno». *Some* se emplea en las oraciones afirmativas o en las interrogativas para ofrecer o pedir algo. *Any* se usa en la gran mayoría de las oraciones interrogativas, en las negativas y en las interrogativas negativas. *No* es una negación y sustituye a todas las otras negaciones que aparecen en la oración.

Adjetivos posesivos

Los adjetivos posesivos en inglés son *my*, *your*, *his*, *her*, *its*, *our*, *your* y *their*; son invariables, no van precedidos nunca de artículo y concuerdan en género con el poseedor (no con lo poseído). Se usan mucho en inglés; sustituyen al artículo delante de los nombres de familiares, las partes del cuerpo, las prendas de vestir y los objetos personales.

Adverbios

En inglés, unos adverbios tienen forma propia, otros tienen la misma que el adjetivo y algunos se componen añadiendo el sufijo *-ly* al adjetivo. No se puede formar un adverbio a partir de un adjetivo que termina en *-ly*; en estos casos se puede emplear la expresión *in a... way* / *manner* o bien un adverbio de significado afín.

Adverbios de modo

Modifican al verbo; generalmente terminan en *-ly* y se colocan al final de la oración (sujeto + verbo + adverbio). Nunca se sitúan entre el verbo y el complemento.

Adverbios de tiempo y de lugar

Estos adverbios se colocan siempre al principio o al final de la oración.

Adverbios de frecuencia

Indican la frecuencia con que tiene lugar una acción. Normalmente van delante del verbo, pero con el verbo *to be* se colocan detrás, y con los tiempos verbales compuestos, tras el verbo auxiliar.

Adverbios de cantidad

Sirven para reforzar o debilitar el significado de un adjetivo, de un verbo o de otro adverbio. Preceden al adjetivo o al adverbio al cual modifican, excepto *enough*, que se coloca detrás. Cuando los adverbios de cantidad modifican al verbo, lo preceden, y se colocan entre este y el sujeto, excepto *much*, *a lot*, *a bit* y *a little*, que van al final de la oración.

Adverbios fraseológicos

Expresan el punto de vista de quien habla con respecto a lo que está diciendo. Se pueden colocar en cualquier punto de la oración.

Preposiciones

A continuación, enumeramos las principales preposiciones del inglés.

Recordemos que no tienen una traducción literal, por lo que a veces las preposiciones inglesas no coinciden con las españolas.

Preposiciones de tiempo

At: indica la hora o el momento exacto en que ocurre una acción;

On: indica un día de la semana o del mes, y también se emplea con los sustantivos terminados en *-day*.

In: indica meses, estaciones, años y las partes del día (excepto en la expresión *at night*).

By: indica un plazo bien definido.

Within: indica un periodo no definido.

Since: indica el momento preciso en que se inició una acción en el pasado.

For: introduce un periodo de tiempo para señalar cuánto dura una acción.

During: equivale a «durante».

Till / until: indican hasta cuándo se produce una acción.

Before: indica que algo ocurrió antes que otro acontecimiento.

After: indica que algo sucede después de otra acción.

Preposiciones de lugar

In: indica el estado en un lugar o dentro del mismo; se usa para lugares grandes o para ciudades pequeñas, si quien habla vive en ellos; también indica el movimiento dentro de un lugar preciso.

At: indica el estado en un lugar o dentro del mismo; se emplea para lugares pequeños.

On: significa «encima» con contacto.

Between: indica una posición intermedia entre dos cosas o entre dos personas.

Among: indica una posición intermedia entre varias personas o cosas.

In front of: significa «delante de».

Behind: significa «detrás de».

Against: significa «contra».

Under: significa «debajo».

Opposite: significa «enfrente».

Preposiciones de movimiento

To: indica el movimiento hacia un lugar (pero se dice *to go home*, sin ninguna preposición, y *to arrive in / at*, nunca con *to*), aunque este sea en sentido figurado.

Into: indica movimiento desde el exterior hacia el interior.

Though: indica movimiento a través de un lugar, concretamente el paso de un extremo al otro.

Across: indica movimiento a través de un lugar, concretamente por una superficie.

From: indica movimiento desde un lugar, el alejamiento y el origen.

Over: especifica movimiento desde lugar hacia otro, normalmente por encima de una superficie.

By: indica el hecho de moverse cerca / en las proximidades de algo.

Along: indica el hecho de recorrer algo en su longitud.

Around: indica un movimiento circular.

Up: indica movimiento hacia arriba.

Down: indica movimiento hacia abajo.

Under: especifica movimiento por debajo de algo.

Preposiciones de medio

By: se usa con los medios de transporte y de comunicación, y en expresiones como «por mar / por tierra / por aire» *(by sea / by land / by air)*; en cambio, se dice *on foot* («a pie»).

In: se usa cuando el medio de transporte va seguido de un adjetivo posesivo o del nombre del poseedor.

With: se usa para expresar el medio o el instrumento; significa «con».

Without: significa «sin».

Verbos

To be y *to have*

Los verbos *to be* (ser o estar) y *to have* (haber o tener) son los únicos verbos ingleses que tienen un tiempo presente con formas ligeramente distintas. Es conveniente aprenderlas de inmediato para estar en condiciones de componer frases completas en inglés.

	To be (**Ser o estar**)
Singular	*Plural*
I am	*We are*
(Yo soy, yo estoy)	(Nosotros somos, nosotros estamos)
You are	*You are*
(Tú eres, tú estás)	(Vosotros sois, vosotros estáis)
He is	*They are*
(Él es, él está)	(Ellos son, ellos están)

	To have (**Haber o tener**)
Singular	*Plural*
I have	*We have*
(Yo he, yo tengo)	(Nosotros hemos, nosotros tenemos)
You have	*You have*
(Tú has, tú tienes)	(Vosotros habéis, vosotros tenéis)
He has	*They have*
(Él ha, él tiene)	(Ellos han, ellos tienen)

Veamos ahora algunas frases.

> *Ej.: I am strong.*
>   Yo soy fuerte.
>
>   *You are pretty.*
>   Tú eres guapa.
>
>   *He is kind.*
>   Él es amable.

We are good.
Nosotros somos buenos.

You are patient.
Vosotros sois pacientes.

They are tall.
Ellos son altos.

Forma negativa de los verbos *to be* y *to have*

Las formas negativas del verbo *to be* y del verbo *to have* se obtienen al colocar la negación *not* después del verbo:

To be (Ser o estar)

Singular	Plural
I am not	*We are not*
(Yo no soy, yo no estoy)	(Nosotros no somos, nosotros no estamos)
You are not	*You are not*
(Tú no eres, tú no estás)	(Vosotros no sois, vosotros no estáis)
He is not	*They are not*
(Él no es, él no está)	(Ellos no son, ellos no están)

To have (Haber o tener)

Singular	Plural
I have not	*We have not*
(Yo no he [tengo])	(Nosotros no hemos [tenemos])
You have not	*You have not*
(Tú no has [tienes])	(Vosotros no habéis [tenéis])
He has not	*They have not*
(Él no ha [tiene])	(Ellos no han [tienen])

FORMA INTERROGATIVA DE LOS VERBOS *TO BE* Y *TO HAVE*

La forma interrogativa de los verbos *to be* y *to have* se obtiene anteponiendo el verbo al pronombre o al nombre:

To be (SER O ESTAR)

Singular	Plural
Am I?	*Are we?*
(¿Soy yo, estoy yo?)	(¿Somos nosotros?)
	(¿Estamos nosotros?)
Are you?	*Are you?*
(¿Eres tú?)	(¿Sois vosotros?)
(¿Estás tú?)	(¿Estáis vosotros?)
Is he?	*Are they?*
(¿Es él?)	(¿Son ellos?)
(¿Está él?)	(¿Están ellos?)

To have (HABER O TENER)

Singular	Plural
Have I?	*Have we?*
(¿He yo?)	(¿Hemos nosotros?)
(¿Tengo yo?)	(¿Tenemos nosotros?)
Have you?	*Have you?*
(¿Has tú?)	(¿Habéis vosotros?)
(¿Tienes tú?)	(¿Tenéis vosotros?)
Has he?	*Have they?*
(¿Ha él?)	(¿Han ellos?)
(¿Tiene él?)	(¿Tienen ellos?)

Presente de otros verbos

El presente de los verbos ingleses es siempre igual que el infinitivo sin *to*.

Únicamente hay una excepción a esta regla: en la tercera persona del singular se añade una -s (siguiendo las reglas del plural).

TO LOVE (AMAR)

Ej.: You love your parents.
Tú amas a tus padres.

He loves his brother.
Él ama a su hermano.

TO COME (VENIR)

Ej.: I come from Madrid.
Yo vengo de Madrid.

We come from Sevilla.
Nosotros venimos de Sevilla.

My father comes from London.
Mi padre viene de Londres.

TO GO (IR)

Ej.: She goes to England.
Ella va a Inglaterra.

We go to France.
Nosotros vamos a Francia.

You go to America.
Vosotros vais a América.

They go to the cinema.
Ellos van al cine.

TO LIVE (VIVIR)

Ej.: I live in Barcelona.
Yo vivo en Barcelona.

You live in Granada.
Tú vives en Granada.

He lives in Madrid.
Él vive en Madrid.

You live in France.
Tú vives en Francia.

FORMA NEGATIVA: OTROS VERBOS

La forma negativa del presente de todos los verbos, excluyendo los auxiliares, se forma con el verbo auxiliar *to do* y la negación *not,* que se colocan entre el sujeto y el verbo, para añadirles después el infinitivo del verbo principal sin *to*. En la tercera persona, en lugar de *do* se emplea *does*.

Ej.: He does not love his town.
Él no ama su ciudad.

You do not love your parents.
Tú no amas a tus padres.

FORMA INTERROGATIVA: OTROS VERBOS

En esta forma se emplea también el auxiliar *to do*, que precede al sujeto.

Ej.: Do you love your town?
¿Amas tu ciudad?

Do you see that house?
¿Ves aquella casa?

Do you go to Cuenca?
¿Vas a Cuenca?

Does George come today?
¿Viene hoy Jorge?

Pasado

El pasado de los verbos regulares ingleses se forma añadiendo -ed al infinitivo sin *to*.
Es igual en todas las personas.
Los verbos terminados en -e sólo añaden una -d.
En cambio, los verbos integrados por una sola sílaba y terminados en consonante, normalmente doblan la consonante delante de -ed.
Los verbos de dos sílabas que terminan en -l doblan siempre la l delante de ed.

Los verbos que terminan en -y cambian esta última grafía por *i* si a la *y* le precede una consonante.

Ej.: *I loved* (el pasado inglés corresponde a las dos formas españolas)
Yo amé, amaba

I wanted
Yo quise, quería

I stopped (de *to stop*)
Yo me detuve, detenía

I travelled (de *to travel*)
Yo viajé, viajaba

I offered (de *to offer*)
Yo ofrecí, ofrecía

El participio pasado de los verbos regulares es igual que el pasado.

Los verbos irregulares tienen una forma especial de pasado y de participio pasado que es necesario aprender de memoria y que es igual en todas las personas (véanse páginas 53-55).

FORMA NEGATIVA E INTERROGATIVA DEL PASADO

Se obtiene, tanto en los verbos regulares como en los irregulares, igual que en el presente, pero en lugar de *do / does*, se emplea siempre *did*. El verbo principal es siempre como el infinitivo sin la partícula *to*.

Ej.: Did you see my sister last night?
   ¿Viste a mi hermana anoche?

   I did not see your sister.
   No vi a tu hermana.

Futuro

Se forma igual en todos los verbos ingleses: por medio de los dos verbos auxiliares *shall* y *will*, a los que se añade el infinitivo sin *to*. El futuro normal se compone con el auxiliar *shall* en la primera persona singular y plural, y *will* en todas las demás. Se emplea *will* en primera persona cuando se desea subrayar el deseo de hacer algo (en Norteamérica hay tendencia a utilizar siempre *will*).

To love (**AMAR**)

Singular	Plural
I shall (will) love	*We shall (will) love*
Yo amaré	Nosotros amaremos
You will love	*You will love*
Tú amarás	Vosotros amaréis
He will love	*They will love*
Él amará	Ellos amarán

Forma negativa
I shall not love
Yo no amaré

Forma interrogativa
Shall I love?
¿Amaré yo?

Forma interrogativa negativa
Shall I not love?
¿No amaré yo?

Verbos defectivos

Los verbos defectivos son aquellos que carecen de infinitivo y participio y, por consiguiente, de todos los tiempos que se construyen a partir de estas dos formas verbales (como, por ejemplo, el futuro y todos los tiempos compuestos). Pertenecen a esta categoría verbos como *must* (yo debo), *can*, *could* (yo puedo, podía), *will*, *would* (yo quiero, quería), *shall*, *should* (yo debo, debía).

Veamos cuáles son las características principales de estos verbos:

1. En la tercera persona de presente, no añaden la -s.
2. En las formas interrogativa y negativa siguen las reglas de los verbos *ser* y *haber* y, por consiguiente, no se les añade *do* ni *did*.
3. El infinitivo del verbo que eventualmente los sigue no lleva *to*.

Estas reglas se resumen en la siguiente frase:

He must not go.
Él no debe ir.

En efecto, *must*, a pesar de estar en tercera persona, no añade la -s; la frase es negativa y no incluye *does*, y el infinitivo «ir» se traduce simplemente por *go* (en lugar de *to go*).

Ej.: I cannot (contraído: *I can't*).
No puedo.

You must not tell these secrets to everybody.
No debes decir a todos estos secretos.

Could you find a seat in the train?
¿Pudiste encontrar plaza en el tren?

Unfortunately I couldn't but I met a friend of mine at the station, so we had a good time all the same.
Por desgracia no, pero me encontré a un amigo en la estación e igualmente lo pasamos bien.

La forma en *-ing*

Se denomina forma en *-ing* la que se construye añadiendo *-ing* al infinitivo sin *to* y que corresponde al participio y gerundio del castellano.

Ej.: to work (trabajar)   *working*
to play (jugar)   *playing*
to tell (decir)   *telling*

Si un verbo termina en -e, dicha e se omite delante de *-ing*.

Ej.: to come (venir)   *coming*

Se emplea siempre la forma en *-ing* después de las preposiciones *before* (antes), *after* (después), *instead of* (en lugar de), *without* (sin), etc. Únicamente la preposición *to*, que se corresponde con las del castellano «de, a, para», rige un infinitivo.

Verbos irregulares

Infinitivo	*Pasado*	*Participio*
to awake (despertar)	awoke	awaken
to be (ser)	was	been
to bear (generar)	bore	born
to become (convertirse)	became	become
to begin (empezar)	began	begun
to bend (doblar)	bent	bent
to bet (apostar)	bet	bet
to bind (atar)	bound	bound
to bleed (sangrar)	bled	bled
to blow (soplar)	blew	blown
to break (romper)	broke	broken
to bring (traer)	brought	brought
to build (construir)	built	built
to buy (comprar)	bought	bought
to catch (coger)	caught	caught
to choose (escoger)	chose	chosen
to come (venir)	came	come
to cost (costar)	cost	cost
to cut (cortar)	cut	cut
to do (hacer)	did	done
to dream (soñar)	dreamt	dreamt
to drink (beber)	drank	drunk
to drive (conducir)	drove	driven
to eat (comer)	ate	eaten
to fall (caer)	fell	fallen
to feed (alimentar)	fed	fed
to feel (sentir)	felt	felt
to find (encontrar)	found	found
to fly (volar)	flew	flown
to forbid (prohibir)	forbade	forbidden

to forget (olvidar)	forgot	forgotten
to forgive (perdonar)	forgave	forgiven
to freeze (helar)	froze	frozen
to get (obtener)	got	got
to give (dar)	gave	given
to go (ir)	went	gone
to grow (crecer)	grew	grown
to have (haber)	had	had
to hear (escuchar)	heard	heard
to hide (esconder)	hid	hid
to hold (sostener)	held	held
to hurt (herir)	hurt	hurt
to keep (guardar)	kept	kept
to know (conocer)	knew	known
to lay (colocar)	laid	laid
to lead (conducir)	led	led
to leave (dejar)	left	left
to lend (prestar)	lent	lent
to let (permitir)	let	let
to lie (yacer)	lay	lain
to light (iluminar)	lit	lit
to lose (perder)	lost	lost
to make (hacer)	made	made
to mean (significar)	meant	meant
to meet (encontrar)	met	met
to pay (pagar)	paid	paid
to put (poner)	put	put
to read (leer)	read	read
to ride (montar a caballo)	rode	ridden
to rise (despertar)	rose	risen
to run (correr)	ran	run
to say (decir)	said	said
to see (ver)	saw	seen
to sell (vender)	sold	sold
to shine (brillar)	shone	shone
to show (mostrar)	showed	shown
to shut (cerrar)	shut	shut
to sing (cantar)	sang	sung

to sit (sentarse)	*sat*	*sat*
to sleep (dormir)	*slept*	*slept*
to smell (oler)	*smelt*	*smelt*
to speak (hablar)	*spoke*	*spoken*
to spend (gastar, pasar)	*spent*	*spent*
to stand (permanecer de pie)	*stood*	*stood*
to sweep (barrer)	*swept*	*swept*
to swim (nadar)	*swam*	*swum*
to take (tomar)	*took*	*taken*
to teach (enseñar)	*taught*	*taught*
to tell (decir)	*told*	*told*
to think (pensar)	*thought*	*thought*
to understand (comprender)	*understood*	*understood*
to wear (vestir)	*wore*	*worn*
to weep (llorar)	*wept*	*wept*
to write (escribir)	*wrote*	*written*

Anexos

Nombres y adjetivos de nacionalidad

Los adjetivos de nacionalidad en inglés se subdividen en varios grupos:

1. Los que terminan en *-an* o *-ian*.

País/continente	Nacionalidad	País/continente	Nacionalidad
Africa	African	Egypt	Egyptian
America	American	India	Indian
Argentina	Argentinian	Italy	Italian
Austria	Austrian	Mexico	Mexican
Brazil	Brazilian	Norway	Norwegian
Canada	Canadian	Peru	Peruvian

2. Los que terminan en *-ish.*

País	Nacionalidad	País	Nacionalidad
Denmark	Danish	Poland	Polish
England	English	Scotland	Scottish
Finland	Finnish	Spain	Spanish
Ireland	Irish	Sweden	Swedish

3. Los que terminan en -ese.

País	Nacionalidad	País	Nacionalidad
China	Chinese	Portugal	Portuguese
Guyana	Guyanese	Senegal	Senegalese
Japan	Japanese	Vietnam	Vietnamese

4. Los que tienen una forma especial propia.

País	Nacionalidad	País	Nacionalidad
France	French	Madagascar	Madagasy
Germany	German	Switzerland	Swiss
Greece	Greek	Wales	Welsh

Las estaciones y el tiempo

The four seasons are:
Las cuatro estaciones son:

Summer	*Autumn (Fall)*	*Spring*	*Winter*
Verano	Otoño	Primavera	Invierno

Se dice:

in summer	*in autumn*	*in spring*	*in winter*
en verano	en otoño	en primavera	en invierno

Weather: corresponde al español «tiempo» cuando se trata de tiempo atmosférico.

Ej.: What is the weather like?
¿Qué tiempo hace?

The weather is fine.
Hace buen tiempo.

It is hot.
Hace calor.

The weather is dry.
El tiempo es seco.

Today is a sunny day.
Hoy es un día soleado.

Yesterday was a cloudy day.
Ayer fue un día nublado.

In winter it is cold.
En invierno hace frío.

This is a warm day.
Este es un día cálido.

It's a foggy day.
Es un día brumoso.

Los meses

Los meses del año se escriben siempre con mayúscula.

   Ej.: in March   in December

Pero:

   on the seventh of July
   el 7 de julio

Se utiliza *in* delante de los nombres de estaciones meses y fechas expresadas en años.

Se emplea *on* precediendo los nombres de los días de la semana y las fechas expresadas en meses.

Las horas y los días

Las horas en punto se dicen en inglés: *one o'clock, two o'clock*, etc.

Ej.: *It's one o'clock.*   *It's ten o'clock.*
     Es la una.   Son las diez.

     At one o'clock.   *At seven o'clock.*
     A la una.   A las ocho.

Entre la hora en punto y la media hora siguiente, se dice el número de minutos que han pasado de la hora, más *past* y más la hora que ha pasado.

Ej.: *It's twenty past four.*
     Son las cuatro y veinte.
     It's twenty minutes past four.
     Son las cuatro y veinte.

Entre la media hora y la siguiente hora en punto, se dice el número de minutos que faltan para esta, más *to* y más la hora siguiente.

Ej.: *It's ten to nine.*
     Son las nueve menos diez.
     It's ten minutes to nine.
     Son las nueve menos diez.

Los cuartos de hora: los minutos 15 y 45 se expresan con la palabra *quarter* (*past* o *to*).

Ej.: *It's a quarter past seven.*
Son las siete y cuarto.
It's a quarter to eight.
Son las ocho menos cuarto.

La media hora se expresa con *half past* más la hora que ha pasado.

Ej.: *It's half past three.*   Son las tres y media.

La hora digital se dice de otra manera: la hora más los minutos.

Ej.: 9:15 o 21:15   *nine-fifteen (a quarter past nine)*
3:30 o 15:30   *three-thirty (half past three)*
8:10 o 20:10   *eight-ten (ten past eight)*

Los días de la semana se escriben siempre con mayúsculas y son:

Monday	lunes
Tuesday	martes
Wednesday	miércoles
Thursday	jueves
Friday	viernes
Saturday	sábado
Sunday	domingo

Ej.: *Will you meet me at 7:00 on Sunday?*
¿Me puedes esperar el domingo a las siete?

Ejercicios

1. Forme el plural de los siguientes sustantivos:

1. potato ....
2. child ....
3. woman ....
4. experience ....
5. bottle ....
6. knife ....
7. foot ....
8. country ....
9. bus ....
10. lamp ....
11. car ....
12. treasure ....
13. life ....
14. train ....
15. witch ....
16. cross ....
17. wolf ....
18. tooth ....
19. boat ....
20. ear ....

2. Reescriba las siguientes oraciones corrigiendo los errores:

1. Those girls are beautifuls!
   ....

2. He has a dog trained.
   ....

3. This house is old twenty years.
   ....

4. Mark gave her a diamond ring very expensive.
   ....

3. Traduzca al inglés las siguientes frases:

1. He visto un mueble de madera, antiguo, cuadrado y muy grande.
   ....

2. Susan y John tienen dos niños.
   ....

3. Peter tenía una expresión tranquila.
   ....

4. Pasamos el fin de semana en un precioso hotelito en la montaña.
   ....

5. Aquella sopa tenía un sabor horrible.
   ....

6. Mary es una muchacha alta y atractiva.
   ....

7. En el lago he visto muchas barcas veloces.
   ....

8. Bill tiene un trabajo estresante.
   ....

9. Este automóvil tiene quince años.
   ....

10. Las montañas están preciosas en esta época del año.

    ....

4. Complete con *the, a* o *an*:

1. Could you give me .... red pen, please?
2. Did .... lawyer tell you what to do?
3. I went to the police station and asked to talk to .... cop.
4. Did you eat .... cake I made for you?
5. They live in .... old house because they can't afford a new one.
6. .... Colorado river runs through .... Grand Canyon.
7. I'm going to .... post office to buy .... stamp for my letter.
8. I think I need .... new t-shirt.
9. Mark went home .... hour ago.
10. Peter goes to the gym four times .... week.
11. Don't you know that Bill is .... FBI agent?
12. May I offer you .... cup of coffee?
13. Did you read .... magazine I gave you?
14. My father used to be .... architect.
15. Jerry can play .... piano very well.
16. .... car must be insured.
17. .... Amazon forest should be better protected.
18. When I was in London last year I visited .... National Gallery.
19. I'd like to have .... egg for breakfast.

5. Coloque *the* donde sea necesario:

1. .... Atlantic Ocean separates .... Europe from .... America.

2. .... people would rather go to .... sea than to ....
mountains.
3. .... Mary's house is closer than .... mine.
4. .... last month we went to .... Rome and we visited
.... Vatican Museum.
5. .... poor need government help.
6. .... wine is my favourite drink.
7. We live in .... north of Italy.
8. .... Mount Blanc is .... highest mountain in Europe.
9. .... clerk I met at the bank was very rude.
10. .... Earth is .... third planet from .... sun.
11. I like .... classical music.
12. Can you turn off .... television, please?
13. .... blue sweater is mine.
14. .... Republic of Ireland is one of the most beautiful
countries in Europe.
15. .... pandas are in danger of extinction.

6. Coloque *a* o *an* donde sea necesario:

1. Mark works as .... doctor.
2. The speed limit is 120 km .... hour.
3. There is .... elephant at the zoo.
4. There was .... happiness in that family.
5. We need to buy .... milk and .... flour to prepare ....
cake.
6. What .... lovely girl she is!
7. There is .... wisdom in her words.
8. Jerry goes to see his grandparents twice .... week.
9. Susan and John live in .... attic in New York.
10. I've been waiting for you for half .... hour.
11. I'm telling you this as .... mother.
12. Is there .... wine in the fridge?
13. He is .... very wealthy lawyer now.

14. Did you know he has .... twin sister?
15. Last week I had .... exam.

7. Traduzca al inglés:

1. A la gente le gusta el esquí.
2. Mi libro está en la mesa.
3. Si sales, ponte la chaqueta.
4. ¡Vaya coche!
5. Las Montañas Rocosas se encuentran en Estados Unidos.
6. Susan es profesora.
7. Las manzanas cuestan 1 euro el kilo.
8. El perro de John es muy divertido.
9. El Everest es la montaña más alta del mundo.
10. El tenis es mi deporte favorito.

8. Complete con *a / an, the* o *some*:

1. I have to go to the supermarket to buy .... bread, ...
   wine and .... packet of sugar.
2. Mark wanted .... information from you.
3. He is looking for .... job.
4. We had .... exciting vacation last week.
5. John gave me .... book to read, but I didn't like it.
6. .... movie we saw last night was very entertaining.
7. If you want there is .... milk over there.
8. .... children are playing in the back yard.
9. I'd like to have .... tea, thanks.
10. I think everybody needs .... happiness.

9. Traduzca al inglés usando el genitivo sajón:

1. El coche de Mark es muy veloz.
2. El hijo de Susan es mi amigo.

3. ¿Has comprado el periódico de hoy?
4. La muñeca de Mary está rota.
5. La casa de Bill y Maura es grande.
6. Esto no es asunto de nadie.
7. El coche de sus padres está en el garaje.
8. El autobús de los estudiantes es amarillo.
9. Susan es la esposa de John.
10. El viaje de Emily es largo.

10. Complete las siguientes oraciones con *there is / are, it's* o *they're*:

1. .... a dog in your yard. .... big!
2. .... many people in the garden. .... all Mark's friends.
3. .... an interesting movie on television and .... funny too.
4. Today .... a beautiful day. .... no clouds in the sky!
5. .... many books in this room and .... all Mary's.

11. Complete las oraciones con *as... as... o not as... as...* y uno de los siguientes adjetivos:

soon - bad - good - annoying - intelligent - fast - tall - easy - far - white

1. It took us only 30 minutes to arrive: it isn't .... we thought.
2. They need the job done quickly. I'll finish it .... I can.
3. She is almost giving birth to the baby: you must drive .... possible!
4. «Are you .... your sister?» «No, I'm taller.»
5. I'm very disappointed because the dinner we had today was .... it was yesterday.

6. He isn't .... his brother, is he?
7. He got so scared that he was .... a sheet!
8. Pay attention because learning English is .... you think.
9. Her husband is so boring: he is .... anybody can be.
10. Stealing a car is .... killing someone.

12. Complete las oraciones con el comparativo de los siguientes adjetivos y adverbios:

difficult - efficient - crowded - early - good - slowly - old - far - bad - fast

1. A Ferrari is .... than a Fiat.
2. The exam was .... than I hoped: it was very hard to pass it.
3. The concert was a big success: the theatre was .... then we expected.
4. Jane is studying hard and I think her Italian is getting ....
5. York is .... than Lincoln or Selby.
6. Alice is .... than her husband: she was born in '70, he was born in '73.
7. The new hospital is .... than the old one.
8. Mark injured himself and the cut was .... than he thought so he had to go to the hospital.
9. Peter will have to get up .... than usual because his flight is at 8 a.m.
10. Could you please drive ....?

13. Formule las preguntas correctamente empleando el superlativo relativo de superioridad:

Ej.: Who / tall / guy / your classroom?
Who is the tallest guy in your classroom?

1. Soccer / popular / sport / Spain?

....

2. Which / beautiful / city / your country?

....

3. Who / annoying / person / you / ever met?

....

4. Brad Pitt / famous / actor / USA?

....

5. What / wild / thing / Peter / ever done?

....

6. What / exciting / holiday / you / ever had?

....

7. Mark / funny / person / your family?

....

8. Queen / wealthy / woman / U.K.?

....

9. *Avatar* / entertaining / movie / you / ever seen?

....

10. Everest / high / mountain / the world?

....

14. Traduzca al inglés las siguientes oraciones:

1. Henry cree que es menos inteligente que su hermano Robert.

....

2. Esta película es menos interesante que la que vi la semana pasada.

....

3. Tu padre es menos alto de lo que pensaba.

....

4. La esposa de Bill es menos bella de lo que se dice.

....

5. Tu gato es menos holgazán que el mío.

....

15. Formule preguntas con las siguientes palabras usando el superlativo relativo de inferioridad:

Ej.: lesson / interesting / day
It's the least interesting lesson of the day.

1. soup / tasty / I / ever eaten
....

2. movie / interesting / we / see / this week
....

3. exam / hard / I / ever done
....

4. Robert / boring / person / his family
....

5. Mary / pretty / girl / her company
....

6. Bill / writer / known / catalogue
....

7. Jim / famous / pilot / his category
....

8. ring / precious / King's collection
....

9. Bob and Lucy / talented / actors / their company
....

10. Jerry / diligent / student / his class
....

16. Traduzca al inglés las siguientes oraciones:

1. Peter tiene una gran colección de sellos.
....

2. Considero que Mark es mi mejor amigo.
....

3. Emily es una anciana muy simpática.

....

4. Robert y Mary estaban muy felices el día de su boda.

....

5. Nos sorprendió mucho verlos juntos.

6. El ladrón huyó en su rapidísimo automóvil.

7. Estaba muy molesto y desconcertado porque mis padres no me creían.

....

8. Ayer vi una joya carísima que me gustaría tener.

....

9. Siempre he pensado que Paul era una persona muy aburrida, pero mi esposa, en cambio, lo considera divertidísimo.

....

10. Russell Crowe es un actor australiano buenísimo.

....

17. Forme oraciones empleando la fórmula comparativo + *and* + comparativo:

Ej.: my job / become / stressful
My job becomes more and more stressful.

1. that singer / get / popular

....

2. since Alice arrived in Italy her Italian / has got / good

....

3. if we don't reduce the traffic / the air / will be polluted

....

4. Jim must study otherwise / he will have / few / possibilities / of graduating

....

5. inflation will increase if / the prices / get / high

....

18. Complete las siguientes oraciones con el pronombre personal correcto:

1. John isn't here. Where has .... gone?
2. I've forgotten the keys. ....'m just going to get them.
3. If .... see Mark and Jerry tell them to come to the party.
4. .... have the suitcases: where can .... put them?
5. Don't invite Bill: .... don't like him.
6. Mary and .... are good friends, but I haven't heard from her in a while.
7. I'm afraid of his dog: ....'s so aggressive!
8. Our car doesn't work: can .... help us?
9. The shark is a really fascinating creature, but .... is also very dangerous.
10. We are her friends: .... should talk to us.

19. Traduzca al inglés las siguientes oraciones:

1. Me llamo Mary y soy profesora.

   ....

2. ¿Dónde has puesto los libros? No los encuentro.

   ....

3. Mi automóvil está estropeado, ¿puedes prestarme el tuyo?

   ....

4. ¿Has visto la película *Titanic*? Creo que la alquilaremos.

   ....

5. ¿Has hablado con Mark? Creo que te está buscando.

   ....

6. Jerry no me gusta: ¡tienes que dejar de verlo!

   ....

7. ¿Puedes ayudarme con los deberes?

   ....

8. ¿Por qué no nos llevas al cine?

   ....

9. ¿Sabes dónde está Susan? Tengo que ir con ella al supermercado.

   ....

10. Los juguetes están en el jardín: ve a buscarlos.

   ....

20. Complete las siguientes frases con un pronombre demostrativo:

1. .... is what you say but I can't believe it!
2. .... is my brother over there.
3. Mark, ... is my friend Bill.
4. .... is my umbrella, ... is yours.
5. .... over there are my dearest friends.
6. You should read ....: it's a beautiful book.
7. .... are not my parents. My parents are .... in the corner of the room.
8. «Which are the trees you planted?» «.......... in the back yard.»
9. Can you put .... on the table, please?
10. .... is my neighbor's dog.

21. Complete las oraciones usando el adjetivo demostrativo que corresponda:

1. .... mountains on the horizon are beautiful.
2. Can you help me? .... bags are so heavy!
3. .... ice-cream is delicious.
4. .... girls here are Italian.
5. I can't go on vacation .... month: I'll go next month.
6. .... boy of yours seems very intelligent.
7. .... people on the porch are my relatives.

8. Bill, is .... pen on my desk over there yours?
9. Put .... apples in .... fridge.
10. .... cartoon is my nephew's favourite.

22. Complete las siguientes oraciones usando *some, any* o *no*:

1. I need .... sugar: do you have ....?
2. Are there .... dogs in the yard?
3. Have Susan and John got .... children?
4. I was at the supermarket buying .... oranges when I remembered we had .... in the fridge.
5. There is .... ice cream left.
6. Hasn't Rob got .... cats?
7. «Can I borrow .... of your books?» «Sure, take .... book you want.»
8. Would you like .... tea or .... coffee?
9. My son doesn't like .... meat: he is a vegetarian.
10. This relationship has .... future: we should finish it.

23. Complete con *anybody* o *anything*:

1. You're free to do .... you like.
2. Did you find .... interesting during your investigation?
3. I didn't meet .... I knew on vacation.
4. Has .... seen Frank?
5. I think .... can go to that party.
6. You can order .... you like.
7. He says he doesn't know .... but I don't believe him.
8. I haven't heard .... from Mary but we are not close friends.
9. Is there .... here?
10. Did you buy .... yesterday?

24. Complete las siguientes oraciones con el pronombre indefinido más adecuado:

1. I have .... in my eye: can you check, please?
2. I thought there was .... at the door but when I opened I found ....
3. I was very disappointed because didn't find .... shoes.
4. I'm afraid we don't have .... to drink in the fridge.
5. Yes, I met .... at the cinema: it was my old friend Alice.
6. She is hiding .... but I still don't know what.
7. There is .... I can do to help you, I'm sorry.
8. .... was interested in his business but he thought .... was spying on him.
9. There is .... there: you're looking in the wrong places.
10. Is there .... wrong? You look so sad.

25. Traduzca al inglés las siguientes oraciones:

1. A muchos de nosotros nos gusta la montaña.

....

2. Mary ha pasado varios días en casa de su hermana.

....

3. Tanto a John como a Susan les gusta mucho jugar a tenis.

....

4. Ninguno de los dos está enfermo.

....

5. Ha venido una tal Alice a buscarte.

....

6. Los imputados son los dos culpables.

....

7. Han sucedido muchas cosas extrañas en esta casa.

....

8. Están todos tristes por la muerte del señor Brown.

....

9. No ha trabajado lo bastante para lograr un ascenso.

....

10. ¡Peter es tan buen chico!

....

26. Complete las siguientes oraciones usando *little, a little, few* o *a few*:

1. «Do you want some milk with your tea?» «.........., please.»
2. Only .... of our customers have accounts.
3. .... town have such beautiful buildings.
4. .... is known about the side effects of this drugs.
5. Only .... people like going to the opera.
6. There was .... time to make that decision.
7. This winter there were only .... days of rain.
8. The boy was .... scared of the dog.
9. I have .... respect for that person.
10. There are very .... discos in this town.

27. Complete las oraciones usando *much, many, a lot (of)* o *several*:

1. He spends .... money gambling.
2. There are .... interesting paintings at the gallery.
3. Is it better to have .... money or .... friends?
4. Can we talk later? I don't have .... time now.
5. .... people saw the accident, not just you.
6. The doctor couldn't do .... for that patient.
7. We don't have .... water: go to the supermarket to buy some bottles.
8. I go to the cinema .... times a week.
9. I have so .... things to do today!
10. The hotel is .... kilometres away, so let's drive.

28. Complete las oraciones usando *either (of)*, *either... or...*, *neither (of)*, *neither... nor...*, *both*, *each* o *every*:

1. Men should shave .... day.
2. .... Mark and Peter were late so we couldn't make it for the movie.
3. We can .... go to the cinema .... stay at home.
4. .... the defendants were found guilty.
5. These sweaters cost £ 30 ....
6. Those movies are horrible: I liked .... them.
7. Since February it's been raining .... week.
8. Can .... of you speak Italian?
9. .... of their dogs has a nice dog-house.
10. .... of them are very good tennis players.

29. Complete las oraciones con el pronombre posesivo correspondiente:

1. Hey, you've lost a bag: is this ....?
2. «Is this Susan's car?» «No, ... is in the garage.»
3. «How are your parents?» «They're fine, thanks. How are ....?»
4. This is your book but I'm desperate because I don't know where I put ....
5. «Are these your shoes?» «No, these are not ....»
6. I've seen your house and the Smith's house: .... has a bigger garden.
7. «This is Jerry's dog!» «No, I'm sure it is not ....»
8. My dog thinks this ball is ....
9. We have met Mary and Bill's children: .... are not so intelligent.
10. We have to share these clothes: this is .... and this is ....

30. Complete las oraciones con el pronombre reflexivo correspondiente:

1. I cut ....
2. Watch ....!
3. We made this furniture ....
4. The Pope .... has visited that church.
5. They don't need your help. They'll do it ....
6. The Queen .... said she liked that movie.
7. Peter blamed .... for the accident.
8. My parents went to London ....
9. I met the President ....
10. We don't need to concern .... with the details of the project.

31. Traduzca al inglés las siguientes oraciones:

1. Se enamoraron el uno del otro nada más verse.

....

2. Nos ayudamos mutuamente cuando es necesario.

....

3. Peter y Mark se acusan mutuamente.

....

4. La madre dice a sus hijos que deben llevarse bien los unos con los otros.

....

5. Él quiso que nos escucháramos unos a otros.

....

32. Complete con un pronombre relativo, siempre que sea necesario:

1. The sport .... I prefer is soccer.
2. The boy .... brings you the newspaper is my brother.

3. The house .... you visited was not mine.
4. Mark is a person .... actions are true to his words.
5. The woman .... you saw him talking to was his sister.
6. Brawn is the team .... won the FI championship last year.
7. This is the town in .... I was born.
8. Robert is the child .... mother died last month.
9. The plane .... I had to catch was two hours late.
10. The film is about a man .... wife cheats on him.

33. Complete las oraciones con el adjetivo posesivo correspondiente:

1. .... name is Mary. What's .... name?
2. .... car has broken down: I have to take it to the mechanic.
3. Mary and Jerry have been together for 10 years: .... marriage is very solid.
4. Put on .... jacket: it is very cold outside.
5. Have you seen .... wallet? I can't find it anywhere.
6. I think that Susan wants to change .... job.
7. A tree loses drops .... leaves in autumn.
8. We are planning to go on vacation with .... friends Susan and John.
9. Thank you for .... concern.
10. I believe that many people are not satisfied with .... lives.
11. Bill, I like .... sweater: where did you buy it?
12. Alice is English but .... boyfriend Alain is French.
13. A happy dog wags .... tail.
14. Susan and Elizabeth are with .... husbands.
15. .... friends will come to visit us next summer.

34. Construya oraciones ordenando correctamente las palabras:

1. what / do / often / they / read
   ....

2. always / Mark / wins / at tennis
   ....

3. shelf / high / is / too / the
   ....

4. this food / excellent / is / absolutely
   ....

5. weather / fortunately / good / is / the
   ....

6. Peter / his car / very / drives / carefully
   ....

7. sometimes / go to / we / the cinema
   ....

8. homework / did / easily / their / they
   ....

9. go to / I / twice / the gym / a week
   ....

10. won / yesterday / almost / we / the lottery
    ....

35. Traduzca las siguientes oraciones al inglés:

1. Siempre me ha gustado la música jazz.
   ....

2. Desgraciadamente no logré convencerle.
   ....

3. Cambió de calle rápidamente para no encontrarse con Mary.
   ....

4. Siempre he hecho mi trabajo solo.
   ....

5. Por favor, siéntate en silencio unos minutos y te lo explico todo.

....

6. El castillo de arena que construimos con esfuerzo cayó al cabo de diez minutos.

....

7. ¡No os lo podré agradecer bastante!

....

8. Jerry está a dieta, pero todavía come demasiado.

....

9. Susan habla francés correctamente.

....

10. Alice todavía no ha terminado sus deberes.

....

36. Reescriba las oraciones colocando el adverbio en el lugar correcto:

1. I have done always what I believe in strongly.

....

2. I haven't yet written the letter.

....

3. Mark loves still Lucy.

....

4. Do you go to the cinema often?

....

5. I say always what I think.

....

6. We didn't like very much Madonna's last album.

....

7. Susan and John live here no longer.

....

8. Have you had lunch already?

....

9. Mary believed truly in what she was doing.

....

10. This box isn't enough big.

....

37. Complete las oraciones con uno de los adverbios de modo de la lista:

loudly - slowly - high - hard - easily

1. We .... climbed the hill.
2. I can't stand them: they speak so ....!
3. She drives so .... that she's got a fine!
4. It was snowing .... last night and now there are 10 cm of snow on the ground.
5. Cliffs stand .... above the ocean.

38. Complete las oraciones con uno de los adverbios de tiempo y de lugar de la lista:

yet – already – someday – tomorrow – behind – yesterday – anywhere – someplace – over there – still

1. I can't come home for dinner because we are .... at the meeting.
2. I haven't decided what to do ....
3. Can you put this book on the table ....?
4. We will go to visit our grandparents ....
5. You can keep the magazine: I have .... read it.
6. Runners must run fast or be left .... by the others.
7. Jim thinks that .... he will be famous.
8. Mary left her purse .... but she can't remember where.
9. .... I went to school even though I was sick.
10. I can't find them ....!

39. Complete las oraciones usando uno de los adverbios de frecuencia de la lista:

usually - never - always - seldom - ever

1. I .... go to the theatre: I go two or three times a year.
2. .... they come home at 6 p.m. but today they had a meeting with their boss.
3. Have you .... ridden a horse?
4. Susan and John .... go to the sea for their vacation.
5. I know I should take exercise but I .... do it: I'm too lazy.

40. Complete las oraciones usando uno de los adverbios de cantidad de la lista:

almost - really - much - only - enough

1. He couldn't pass the exam because he didn't study ....
2. Wait five minutes: I've .... finished my homework.
3. Mark doesn't trust anybody else with his car: he .... lends it to me.
4. Elizabeth was sick yesterday but now she feels .... better.
5. Peter didn't like the movie but I .... enjoyed it.

41. Complete las oraciones usando uno de los adverbios fraseológicos de la lista:

probably - unfortunately - perhaps - surely - definitely

1. He was .... drunk and that caused him to drive off the road.

2. Mary was .... there; there is no doubt about it.
3. .... I'll go out with my friends tonight; I'm not sure yet.
4. .... the weather is not good for a picnic.
5. .... you don't believe that nonsense.

42. Traduzca al inglés las siguientes oraciones:

1. Por favor, ¿podrías hablar más lentamente?
....
2. Susan ha corrido más rápido que los demás.
....
3. Han jugado peor que la semana anterior.
....
4. Mark y Peter bajaron por la colina cada vez más deprisa.
....
5. No puedo caminar tan deprisa como tú.
....

43. Complete las oraciones con *in*, *on* o *at*:

1. Peter's birthday is .... the 14th of September.
2. Susan can't talk to you: she's having a shower .... the moment.
3. They usually go to church .... Sundays.
4. Her contract expires .... the beginning of March.
5. .... two days we are going to visit our cousins in Liverpool.
6. We are late! The movie starts .... 8.30.
7. What are you going to do .... New Year's Eve?
8. We like going out .... night.
9. They always go on vacation .... August.
10. Susan and John are planning to move .... four weeks.

44. Complete las siguientes oraciones con *during, for* o *since*:

1. .... the meeting, she received a phone call and left the room.
2. His parents have been married .... 1962.
3. I have been in Washington .... two weeks.
4. My partner and I have been working together .... almost five years.
5. Mary's husband fell asleep .... the opera.
6. After the fight my brother and his friend didn't talk .... a week.
7. Alice and Peter haven't seen each other .... her birthday party.
8. .... the lesson he was reading a comic book.
9. I haven't seen any snow .... I moved to California.
10. My sister has lived in Miami .... five years.

45. Complete las oraciones con *at* o *in*:

1. I think that mom is .... the kitchen.
2. Peter is .... hospital after he fell from the ladder.
3. I left my bag .... your car.
4. Elizabeth is staying .... her mother's house.
5. We had dinner .... a very fancy restaurant last night.
6. My parents are .... the living-room watching television.
7. Was Mark .... home last week end?
8. The table is .... the middle of the dining-room.
9. Jerry just called: he is .... the station waiting for you.
10. Susan lived .... Italy for 2 years.

46. Complete las oraciones con *to, into* o *from*:

1. My parents go .... the theatre twice a month.
2. I received a book .... Mark.

3. Mary put the watch .... its box.
4. Alice and Emily went .... Australia for their vacation.
5. Peter went .... his office to look for my notebook.
6. I thought he was at school but he went .... the park.
7. Where does Susan come ....?
8. We walked down the street and .... the movie theatre.
9. This letter is .... my sister.
10. That highway leads .... Los Angeles.

47. Traduzca al inglés las siguientes frases:

1. ¿Este regalo es para mí?

....

2. El gato está encima de la silla, no debajo.

....

3. «¿De dónde vienes?». «Vengo de Canadá».

....

4. Los señores Brown siempre son amables con nosotros.

....

5. No tememos a Jerry.

....

6. Intenté pasar por la puerta, pero estaba cerrada con llave, por eso entré por la ventana del salón.

....

7. Me mudé de Londres a Dublín.

....

8. Queríamos ir a la ciudad en tren, pero lo perdimos y tuvimos que ir en coche.

....

9. Nunca voy a la oficina en autobús, voy siempre a pie.

....

10. Llegamos a Cardiff a las 4 de la tarde.

....

48. Complete las oraciones con *by, within* o *till / untill*:

1. Mark will be in London .... next weekend.
2. I will finish this report .... 6 p.m.
3. We can't work again .... Monday.
4. You must do the exam .... the end of the month.
5. The bill is due .... 30 days.
6. Mary will tell me .... Tuesday if she'll come to the mountains with us.
7. .... you live here you'll do what I say!
8. Peter must wake up .... 7 o'clock.
9. .... I get the money due to me, I can't pay you.
10. .... the end of July I'll have read all those books.

49. Complete las oraciones con *across, through, over* o *under*:

1. There is a bridge .... the river.
2. The ice cracked .... his feet.
3. Thieves entered my house .... the window.
4. Roots are .... the soil.
5. We walked .... her garden to reach Peter's house.
6. The biologist looked .... her binoculars to see birds.
7. All those employees are .... her management.
8. Peter and Liz live .... the road.
9. A cloud of smoke rose .... the town.
10. The train went .... a long tunnel.

50. Escriba las siguientes oraciones en forma negativa e interrogativa:

1. Mary is afraid of dogs.

....

2. We are happy.

....

3. He is hungry.

....

4. They are bored.

....

5. You are sorry.

....

51. Complete las oraciones conjugando correctamente el verbo *to be* junto con uno de los adjetivos de la lista:

mad - ill - interested - sleepy - happy - upset - cheap - cold - sad - fine

1. Alice .... because her boyfriend left her.
2. Yesterday Susan .... so she went to the doctor.
3. Mark is going to bed because he ....
4. Why .... you .... at me?
5. I need my coat: it .... outside.
6. Last week Peter and Jerry .... because they found a good job.
7. .... they .... in fine arts?
8. Robert .... by the bad news.
9. Don't worry: I ....!
10. The hotel room .... so we could afford to stay an extra night.

52. Complete las oraciones conjugando correctamente la construcción *to have got*:

1. .... you .... a dog?
2. Susan .... two brothers.

3. Robert .... many friends because he is boring.
4. I'd like to go on vacation, but I .... any money.
5. .... John .... a new car? No, he ....
6. I .... bad headache today.
7. How much money .... with you?
8. We .... the book you needed, but we sold it.
9. .... Susan and John .... any children?
10. I .... a pen so I can't write.

53. Complete las oraciones con la fórmula *to have* (conjugada en el tiempo correcto) + una de las palabras de la lista:

beer – fight – fun – talk – dinner – nap – picnic – holiday – quarrel – shower

1. I'm dirty. I'm going to ....
2. We .... at the pub before going home.
3. Mark and John don't look at each other because they .... last night.
4. The movie was very boring and we ....
5. I'm .... with Susan at the restaurant on the corner.
6. My brother and I .... an interesting .... yesterday. We hadn't talked like that since we were kids.
7. I'm very tired. I think I'm going to .... after dinner.
8. Since today is a beautiful day we .... in our yard at the moment.
9. Peter and Liz are pretty stressed: they should ....
10. They always .... when they have to decide to go on vacation.

54. Traduzca las siguientes oraciones utilizando la fórmula *have* + objeto + participio pasado:

Ej.: He hecho pintar la casa. - *I had my house painted.*

1. He llevado el coche a lavar.
   ....

2. Ayer me cortaron el pelo.
   ....

3. No puedo invitarte a comer porque me están pintando la casa.
   ....

4. ¿Mark ha llevado el coche a arreglar?
   ....

5. ¿Haces limpiar las ventanas cada mes?
   ....

6. Nos están construyendo un garaje nuevo.
   ....

7. Mientras me estaba cortando el pelo, la policía se llevó mi coche.
   ....

8. A Peter le arrancarán un diente.
   ....

9. Les están limpiando la bodega.
   ....

10. ¿Os han instalado la antena nueva?
   ....

55. Complete las oraciones utilizando la forma correcta de los siguientes verbos:

watch - get up - want - be - jog - eat - go - speak - like - work

1. We usually .... at 6.00 a.m.
2. Mary .... a soap opera every day.
3. My husband .... as a lawyer.

4. I .... glad to be here.
5. «........................ she .... flowers?» «No, she doesn't.»
6. Alice .... to go to the cinema but her boyfriend doesn't.
7. Peter .... around the park every day to be in shape.
8. What .... you .... for dinner?
9. Robert .... to school by bus.
10. Susan .... Italian very well.

56. Construya oraciones interrogativas usando el *present simple*:

1. Jim / teach / English / well?
   ....
2. The boy / want / to stay / here with us?
   ....
3. You / study / at the university?
   ....
4. Mark / often / reply / to your letters?
   ....
5. Alice / not / go / to school?
   ....
6. They / want / to go / to the sea?
   ....
7. They / not / like / swimming?
   ....
8. Peter / not / like / his job?
   ....
9. You / not / see / the roses over there?
   ....
10. Peter and Mark / play / tennis / every week?
    ....

57. Complete las oraciones con el *present continuous* de los verbos de la lista:

live - rain - move out - write - go - read - sit - watch - do - talk

1. He .... in America now.
2. Susan .... to a friend at the moment.
3. .... you .... a letter?
4. You don't need the umbrella because .... now.
5. My grandmother .... her favourite TV show.
6. John and Susan .... of their house tomorrow.
7. What .... Jerry .... in the garden?
8. Peter and Liz .... for a vacation next weekend.
9. I .... a play by Shakespeare.
10. Why .... you .... at my desk?

58. ¿*Present simple o present continuous*? Subraye la forma correcta:

1. «What **are you doing / do you do** for a living?» «I'm a screen writer but I **am not working / don't work** at the moment.»
2. Mary **is liking / likes** swimming so much that she **is swimming / swims** every day.
3. Mark usually **is going to / goes to** work by bus but today he **is going / goes** by car.
4. Can you phone later? Mary **is taking / takes** a bath now.
5. I **am not understanding / don't understand** what she **is saying / says**: her English is so bad!
6. Jerry **isn't knowing / doesn't know** what he **is doing / does**!
7. You **aren't owing / don't owe** me anything.

8. I think that Robert and Alice **are going to / go to** Miami this week-end.
9. Today I **am bathing / bath** the baby.
10. Liz **is meeting / meets** Peter tonight. He **is taking / takes** her to a jazz club.
11. He usually **is wearing / wears** earphones in order no to disturb his parents while they **are watching / watch** TV.
12. «... then suddenly a bomb **is exploding / explodes** and Tom Cruise **is jumping / jumps** out of the window...»
13. I **am not believing / don't believe** you because you **are always lying / always lie!**
14. My son **is wanting / wants** an ice-cream.
15. He **is not working / doesn't work** on Sundays.

59. ¿*Present simple* o *present continuous*? Corrija los posibles errores de las siguientes oraciones:

1. Kids play (..........) in the yard right now.
2. He is knowing (..........) very well what he's doing.
3. I'm reading (..........) a very interesting thriller.
4. This book belongs (..........) to Peter.
5. What are you thinking (..........) about now?
6. Mark always works (..........) at night.
7. She is loving (..........) skiing so much!
8. I play (..........) tennis with Robert tomorrow.
9. Peter usually isn't watching (..........) television in the afternoon.
10. I'm leaving (..........) my house in two days.

60. Complete las oraciones usando los verbos regulares de la lista en *past simple*:

play - live - study - rain - decide - die - invited - enjoy - watch - arrive

1. We .... a great movie last night.
2. Mark .... basketball with his friends yesterday afternoon.
3. Alice .... very hard to prepare her thesis.
4. For their last vacation they .... to travel all around France.
5. Yesterday it .... very hard so my friend and I couldn't play tennis.
6. Mary and her husband .... in that house until three months ago.
7. I .... Susan and John at the party.
8. We .... in time to take the last train.
9. I really .... the play we saw last week.
10. Unfortunately his wife .... six month ago.

61. Complete las oraciones usando los siguientes verbos irregulares en *past simple*:

send - drink - see - go - leave - keep - have - sleep - feel - buy

1. Two days ago we .... a new car.
2. Yesterday I .... a telegram to my friend in York.
3. Yesterday at the party they .... playing the same song!
4. Last Saturday Mary .... to visit her grandparents.
5. Last night I didn't go out because I .... dizzy.
6. When I was a child I .... a red bicycle.
7. At his bachelor party last Wednesday he .... too much beer.
8. I .... him because he was such an idiot!
9. I .... on the coach last night.
10. Last night we .... that friend of yours at the theatre.

62. Forme oraciones correctas empleando verbos en *present perfect*:

Ej.: I / be / England / twice - I have been to England twice.

1. You / ever / meet / my sister?
   ....

2. They / not / finish / their work / yet
   ....

3. It / not / snow / much / this year
   ....

4. Susan / ever / spend / a holiday / in the mountains?
   ....

5. Peter / never / buy / a red car
   ....

6. Your brother / work / ever?
   ....

7. Robert / not / call / back?
   ....

8. Today / Alice / go / to school?
   ....

9. I / often / talk / to Jim
   ....

10. Where / you / be / today?
    ....

63. Construya oraciones interrogativas o interrogativas negativas con el verbo en *past simple*:

Ej.: You / go / school / yesterday - Did you go to school yesterday?

1. You / know / her father died?
   ....

2. He / pay / his employees / last week?

....

3. Jim and Peter / not / go / school / together / when they were kids?

....

4. You and Susan / play / tennis / last Saturday?

....

5. She / not / tell / you / to shut up?

....

6. Your parents / like / the new neighborhood?

....

7. Robert / not / yesterday / speak to his brother?

....

8. I / not / give / you / back / your books?

....

9. When / we / meet him?

....

10. What / you / ask / me?

....

64. ¿*Past simple* o *present perfect*? Elija la forma correcta y subráyela:

1. Yesterday I **went / have gone** shopping.
2. We just **met / have just met** him.
3. When **did you see / have you seen** his friend?
4. Robert **played / has played** tennis at Wimbledon in 1989.
5. **Did you ever travel / Have you ever travelled** by plane?
6. I **didn't read / haven't read** *The Lord of the Rings* yet.
7. **Have you seen / did you see** Susan today?
8. In 2005 Peter **decided / has decided** to learn how to play the piano.
9. We **were here / have been** here for 8 months.
10. **Have you ever been / did you ever go** to Paris?

65. Decida en qué orden ocurrieron los hechos de la lista. Escriba dos oraciones usando *after* + el verbo en *past perfect*:

Ej.: The man looked carefully.
He went into his house.
He crossed the street.
After the man had looked carefully he crossed the street.
After he had crossed the street he went into his house.

1. I went to the airport.
   I got up at 6 a.m.
   I took my flight.
2. Susan went to the post office.
   She sent a letter.
   She bought a stamp.
3. The cop interviewed the people involved in the accident.
   He went to the scene of the accident.
   He arrested the man who was driving.
4. We made an appointment to see the new house.
   We bought the house.
   We went to see the house.
5. Alice read the book.
   She went to the library to take out *Sense and Sensibility*.
   She took the book back to the library.

66. Construya oraciones correctas con los verbos en *past simple* y *past continuous*:

Ej.: I / driving / car / engine / break down - I was driving the car when the engine broke down.

1. Alice / having / shower / Peter / come into / bathroom

....

2. I / watching / soccer match / Robert / call

....

3. Mark and Jerry / having / coffee / see / Jim / with / they / his girlfriend

....

....

4. My parents / sleeping / burglar / break into / house

....

5. I / talking / with the boss / very fast / Liz / leave / new / office

....

....

6. We / playing / tennis / start / to rain

....

7. Mary / driving / cat / cross / street

....

8. I / leaving / house / phone / ring

....

9. My friends / having / party / fire / started

....

10. He / skiing / break / his leg

....

67. Complete las oraciones usando la forma del *present perfect continuous* de los verbos de la siguiente lista:

watch - talk - read - study - work

1. Peter .... in this office since 1999.
2. I .... this book all day.
3. We .... the movie for two hours.
4. Susan .... to her friends for ten minutes.
5. How long .... he .... maths?

68. Complete las oraciones usando la forma del _past perfect continuous_ de los verbos de la siguiente lista:

deliver - study - walk - work - wait

1. Susan felt very tired last night because she .... since 7 a.m.
2. How long .... you .... when I arrived?
3. .... Robert .... milk for 3 years before he got this job?
4. I fell asleep on the couch because I .... for six hours.
5. We .... for an hour when it started to rain.

69. ¿_Present perfect_ o _present perfect continuous_? Elija la forma correcta y complete las oraciones:

1. I .... (to own) this car for 10 years.
2. Susan .... (to drive) her car for 6 months.
3. I'm so sorry I'm late. .... (to wait) for long?
4. How long .... you .... (to know) that?
5. Mark .... (to sleep) since 9 p.m.

70. Traduzca las siguientes oraciones empleando _used to_:

1. Hace años solía hacer _jogging_.
   ....
2. ¿Jugabas a tenis cuando eras más joven?
   ....
3. El año pasado no veníamos a este local.
   ....
4. De joven, ¿Mark era actor?
   ....

5. Hace años vivíamos en esta casa.

....

71. Complete las oraciones con *will* o *won't*:

1. Don't call me tonight. I .... be home.
2. We don't think Mary .... get the promotion. She hasn't worked well.
3. We .... miss the movie if you don't hurry up!
4. «Do you think they .... help us?» «I'm sure they ....»
5. I .... take my son to the dentist tomorrow.
6. Peter and Robert .... go on vacation next week because they have too much work to do.
7. Next Saturday we .... play tennis with Susan and John.
8. It's too late now: I don't think Jerry .... come.
9. It .... rain today: the sun is shining brightly.
10. «Will you go to Mary's party?» «No, I probably .... go because I'm sick.»

72. Conjugue los verbos que hay entre paréntesis en *future continuous*:

1. This time next month we *(leave)* .... for Sydney.
2. I'm sure Mark *(not / watch)* .... TV right now.
3. At this time next Saturday I *(visit)* .... my friends in London.
4. We *(eat)* .... with you in a couple of hours.
5. Tomorrow night I *(wear)* .... that red dress you love so much.
6. Alice is a nurse so she *(work)* .... her night shift next Monday.
7. I *(wait)* .... for you at the post office.

8. When you arrive Peter *(fix)* .... his car in the garage.
9. *(stay)* .... you .... late at work tomorrow?
10. Next week I *(not / wash)* .... the dishes!

73. Conjugue los verbos que hay entre paréntesis en *future perfect* o *future perfect continuous*:

1. I have some work to do but I *(finish)* .... it by 7 p.m.
2. By next April we *(be)* .... married for 7 years.
3. I *(not / finish)* .... the book by this weekend.
4. I know Jim: he *(spend)* .... all that money in a week.
5. By next month Mark *(transfer)* .... to his new office.
6. By December Robert *(work)* .... as a doctor in this hospital for 8 years.
7. In January I started to save money: I hope that by the end of the year I *(save)* .... enough money to buy a new car.
8. Jerry is confident that by next month they *(find)* .... the house of their dreams.
9. By the end of this semester he *(study)* .... here for 4 years.
10. By the end of next month Susan *(teach)* .... in this school for 6 months.

74. Formule una pregunta y respóndala usando el verbo *can / can't*:

Ej.: she / skate (yes) - Can she skate? Yes, she can.

1. he / sing *(yes)*

....

2. they / drive *(no)*

....

3. you / speak French *(yes)*

....

4. we / ride a bike *(yes)*

....

5. she / dance *(no)*

....

6. you / play the guitar *(no)*

....

7. they / have a dog *(yes)*

....

8. he / use a computer *(no)*

....

9. she / play cards *(no)*

....

10. we / run fast *(yes)*

....

75. Complete las oraciones con *can* o *can't*:

1. He .... drive because he is too young.
2. She .... see the movie only if she has the money.
3. On Sundays I .... stay up late.
4. If you feel sick, you .... study well.
5. They .... get along with him: he is so superficial!
6. The doctor .... inject the medicine into the patient because he is so afraid of the needles.
7. We .... play the piano because my mom taught us.
8. The little boy .... tie his own shoes now.
9. You .... eat in the library.
10. We .... bring our dog into the restaurant.

76. Traduzca las siguientes oraciones utilizando el verbo modal *may*:

1. ¿Puedo beber un vaso de agua?
   ....
2. ¿Puedo usar el baño, por favor?
   ....
3. ¿Puedo sentarme aquí, por favor?
   ....
4. ¿Puedo abrir la ventana?
   ....
5. Mary, ¿me concedes este baile?
   ....

77. Traduzca las siguientes oraciones usando *may* o *may not*:

Ej.: Jane puede venir esta noche. - *Jane may come tonight.*

1. Podemos no ir al cine esta noche.
   ....
2. Susan y John pueden comprarse una casa nueva.
   ....
3. Lucy puede no casarse el próximo año.
   ....
4. Él nos puede ayudar.
   ....
5. Ellos pueden no llegar tarde esta noche.
   ....

78. Complete con *must* o *mustn't* y uno de los verbos de la lista:

respect - feed - drive - study - smoke - take - find - repair - go - talk

1. You .... the speed limit.
2. He .... here: it's a hospital!
3. Rick .... because he has an exam next week.
4. If we want to arrive in time, we .... the car.
5. She .... without wearing her glasses.
6. You and your sister .... the cat!
7. Mr. Carter .... the fence: his dog always escapes.
8. The doctor .... to anybody about his patient's disease.
9. I .... to the supermarket: I need some sugar.
10. This little girl is lost: we .... her parents.

79. Traduzca usando el verbo modal *shall*:

1. ¿Tenemos que ponernos las gafas?

....

2. ¿Debo encender la luz?

....

3. ¿Debemos ir al supermercado?

....

4. ¿Tengo que bajar el volumen?

....

5. ¿Debo coger el teléfono?

....

80. Complete las oraciones con *should* o *shouldn't*:

1. We .... put our coats on: it's so cold here!
2. Mary .... have opened the letter: it wasn't addressed to her.
3. When you drive you .... be wearing your seatbelt.
4. The emergency exit door .... be locked.
5. To become a better pianist Mark .... practice more.

6. There .... be another glass on the table.
7. Peter .... watch so much TV: it's a bad habit.
8. They .... have studied more to pass the exam.
9. Mr. Brown thinks his son .... accept the job I've offered him: the salary is good.
10. Brian .... drive so fast: it's dangerous.

81. Complete las siguientes oraciones con *could* o *couldn't*:

1. When I was young I .... run faster than anybody.
2. .... you come a little earlier?
3. Lucy .... get another job if she tried.
4. You .... have told me before, now I have another date.
5. The books have disappeared! Who .... have taken them?
6. Mark .... lend you the money: he is so wealthy.
7. When we met he was so shy that he .... look at me.
8. Peter wanted to go out, but .... because he had to study.
9. .... Mary and Jane do this job by themselves?
10. I .... see because I broke my glasses.

82. Complete las oraciones con *might (have)* o *mightn't (have)*:

1. John said he .... rent a car.
2. Jane .... told me she was married!
3. If you invited Mark, he .... come.
4. Mary told me she .... emigrate.
5. You .... fallen! Watch your steps!
6. Mr and Mrs Brown know they .... wait at the station.
7. He .... told his wife that he wanted to buy a new car.

8. They .... gone out because they don't answer the phone.
9. Susan .... arrive in time if she doesn't go faster.
10. Elizabeth .... buy a new computer because she has no money.

83. Complete conjugando correctamente los verbos *must, have to* y *need*:

1. Do you .... be so rude?
2. You .... quit smoking!
3. Peter .... to relax more: he is so stressed.
4. We .... to go if we don't want to.
5. He .... work harder to get the promotion.
6. In this office even the senior staff .... be at their desks by 9.00.
7. You .... make four copies: two are not enough.
8. I .... wait 15 minutes because Angela was late.
9. We .... pay because John has free tickets.
10. They .... hurry: it's late!

84. Complete conjugando correctamente los verbos *can, may* y *be able to*:

1. Lucy .... come here, but I don't know when.
2. I .... get you a copy if you want one.
3. .... Elizabeth sing?
4. .... I offer you a cup of tea?
5. Susan's baby .... walk by this time next month.
6. We .... see anything in this fog.
7. Maggie .... to help you in a few days.
8. I .... take these library books back tomorrow.
9. The book .... be on the shelf.

10. Bobby now .... drive a car: last week he finally got his licence.

85. Complete conjugando correctamente los modales *should, could* o *might*:

1. Mark .... told me sooner.
2. She .... skate when she was a child.
3. They .... allow parking here: the street is too narrow.
4. Mary .... drunk the wine because she had to drive later.
5. You .... lend Dave the money: you .... never get it back.
6. When I was young I .... ride a bike.
7. I .... go out tonight, but I'm not sure.
8. You .... eat the cookies if you don't want to go to the dentist.
9. Ann thinks that it .... rain tomorrow.
10. I .... lift that bag: it was too heavy.

86. Traduzca al inglés las siguientes oraciones:

1. Me desperté repentinamente y vi al ladrón.

....

2. Robert se embriagó y se cayó.

....

3. Mary ha dejado a su chico.

....

4. Hemos escrito una larga carta.

....

5. Sabía que era demasiado tarde.

....

6. Alice se olvida siempre de coger las llaves.

....

7. Ayer durmieron hasta las 11 de la mañana.

....

8. Susan dijo que estaba muy cansada.

....

9. No he leído nunca un libro tan aburrido.

....

10. Se puso el vestido más bonito.

....

87. Complete las oraciones conjugando correctamente los verbos de la lista:

understand - break - strike - find - go - shoot - get - drive - bite - ring - fall

1. Yesterday Peter .... down the stairs and he .... his arm.
2. I have never .... what he says because his English is so bad.
3. Finally I .... my way back to the hotel.
4. We .... across the country on vacation.
5. The car rolled down the hill and .... a tree.
6. Mark has .... the flu.
7. Mary has never .... to Australia.
8. The telephone .... while I was in the shower.
9. The cop .... a bullet in the ceiling.
10. The cat has often .... its owner.

88. Construya oraciones con las siguientes listas de palabras y conjugue el verbo correctamente:

1. Liz / often / forget / to visit me

....

2. Yesterday / I / read / interesting / article

....

3. Last week / we / meet / our cousins

....

4. Jerry / take off / coat / when he entered the house

....

5. Troops / be used / stop / the rebellion

....

6. Robert / make out / he / be / a student looking for a job

....

7. Liz / learn / some American history / in high school

....

8. Last night / they / come home / very late

....

9. Last week / I / keep £ 20 / for me / give / £10 / to my friend

....

10. They / already / choose / the movie to rent

....

89. Complete las siguientes oraciones usando el verbo adecuado en el tiempo correcto:

1. She had already .... that red dress.
2. Susan and John haven't .... home yet.
3. Alice .... chicken with rice for dinner.
4. I have just .... a letter to my friends in Japan.
5. The boat had a hole so it ....
6. He has never .... to offend you with his words.
7. Last week Peter .... his old car to buy a new one.
8. The dish .... when it .... the floor.
9. I .... a wonderful weekend in Dublin.
10. We often .... a fire in the fireplace on cold winter nights.

90. Construya oraciones interrogativas:

Ej.: Make / you / ever / a chocolate cake? - Have you ever made a chocolate cake?

1. Be / you / ever / to Rome?

    ....

2. Choose / they / already / their / house?

    ....

3. Speak / Mark / often / to his sister?

    ....

4. Meet / he / his teacher / yet?

    ....

5. Hide / Peter and Liz / ever / a secret / from each other?

    ....

6. Learn / you / already / the lesson?

    ....

7. Dream / Mary / ever / about me?

    ....

8. Lose / she / ever / her patience?

    ....

9. Sing / ever / you / in the shower?

    ....

10. Do / they / already / their homework?

    ....

Soluciones

1. 1. potatoes. - 2. children. - 3. women. - 4. experiences. - 5. bottles. - 6. knives. - 7. feet. - 8. countries. - 9. buses. - 10. lamps. - 11. cars. - 12. treasures. - 13. lives. - 14. trains. - 15. witches. - 16. crosses. - 17. wolves. - 18. teeth. - 19. boats. - 20. ears.

2. 1. Those girls are beautiful! - 2. He has a trained dog. - 3. This house is twenty years old. - 4. Mark gave her a very expensive diamond ring.

3. 1. I have seen very big, old, squared and wooden furniture. - 2. Susan and John have two beautiful children. - 3. Peter had a calm expression. - 4. We spent the weekend in a nice, little country hotel. - 5. That soup had a terrible taste. - 6. Mary is a beautiful, tall girl. - 7. At the lake I saw a lot of fast boats. - 8. Bill does a stressful job. - 9. This car is fifteen years old. - 10. Mountains are very beautiful in this season.

4. 1. the. - 2. the. - 3. a. - 4. the. - 5. an. - 6. the; the. - 7. the; a. - 8. a. - 9. an. - 10. a. - 11. an. - 12. a. - 13. the. - 14. an. - 15. the. - 16. the. - 17. the. - 18. the. - 19. an.

5. 1. the; //; //. - 2. //; the; the. - 3. //; //. - 4. //; //; the. - 5. the. - 6. //. - 7. the. - 8. //; the. - 9. the. - 10. the; the; the. - 11. //. - 12. the. - 13. the. - 14. the. - 15. //.

6. 1. a. - 2. an. - 3. an. - 4. //. - 5. //; //; a. - 6. a. - 7. //. - 8. a. - 9 an. - 10. an. - 11. a. - 12. //. - 13. a. - 14. a. - 15. an.

7. 1. People love skiing. - 2. My book is on the table. - 3. If you go out, put your coat on. - 4. What a beautiful car! - 5. The Rocky Mountains are in the USA. - 6. Susan is a teacher. - 7. Apples cost 1 € a kilo. - 8. John's dog is very funny. - 9. Everest is the highest mountain in the world. - 10. Tennis is my favourite sport.

8. 1. some; some; a. - 2. some. - 3. a. - 4. an. - 5. a. - 6. the. - 7. some. - 8. the. - 9. some. - 10. some.

9. 1. Mark's car is very fast. - 2. Susan's son is a friend of mine. - 3. Have you bought today's newspaper? - 4. Mary's doll is broken. - 5. Bill and Maura's house is big. - 6. This is nobody's business. - 7. His parents' car is in the garage. - 8. The students' bus is yellow. - 9. John's wife is Susan. - 10. Emily's journey is long.

10. 1. there is; it's. - 2. there are; they're. - 3. there is; it's. - 4. it's; there are. - 5. there are; they're.

11. 1. as far as. - 2. as soon as. - 3. as fast as. - 4. as tall as. - 5. not as good as. - 6. not as intelligent as. - 7. as white as. - 8. not as easy as. - 9. as annoying as. - 10. not as bad as.

12. 1. faster. - 2. more difficult. - 3. more crowded. - 4. better. - 5. further. - 6. older. - 7. more efficient. - 8. worse. - 9. earlier - 10. more slowly.

13. 1. Is soccer the most popular sport in Spain? - 2. Which is the most beautiful city in your country? - 3. Who is the most annoying person you've ever met? - 4. Is Brad Pitt the most famous actor in the USA? - 5. What is the wildest thing Peter has ever done? - 6. What is the most exciting holiday you've ever had? - 7. Is Mark the funniest person in your family? - 8. Is the Queen the wealthest woman in the U.K.? - 9. Is *Avatar* the most entertaining movie you've ever seen? - 10. Is Everest the highest mountain in the world?

14. 1. Henry thinks he is less intelligent than his brother Robert. - 2. This movie is less interesting than the one I saw last week. - 3. Your father is less tall than I thought. - 4. Bill's wife is less beautiful than people said. - 5. Your cat is less lazy than mine.

15. 1. It's the least tasty soup I've ever eaten? - 2. It's the least interesting movie we've seen this week? - 3. It's the least hard exam I've ever done? - 4. Robert is the least boring person in his family? - 5. Mary is the least pretty girl of her company? - 6. Bill is the least known writer of the catalogue? - 7. Jim is the least famous pilot in his category? - 8. This is the least precious ring of the King's collection? - 9. Bob and Lucy are the least talented actors of their company? - 10. Jerry is the least diligent student in his class?

16. 1. Peter has a very big collection of stamps. - 2. I consider Mark my best friend. - 3. Emily is a very nice old lady. - 4. Robert and Mary were very happy on their wedding day. - 5. We were very surprised to see them together. - 6. The thief drove in away on his very fast car. - 7. I was very upset and disconcerted because my parents didn't believe me. - 8. Yesterday I saw a very expensive jewel that I'd like to have. - 9. I've always thought that Paul was a very boring person but my wife considers him very funny. - 10. Russell Crowe is a very good Australian actor.

17. 1. That singer is getting more and more popular. - 2. Since Alice arrived in Italy her Italian has got better and better. -

3. If we don't reduce the traffic the air will be more and more polluted. - 4. Jim must study otherwise he will have fewer and fewer possibilities of graduating. - 5. Inflation will increase if the prices get higher and higher.

18. 1. he. - 2. I. - 3. you. - 4. I; I. - 5. I. - 6. I. - 7. it. - 8. you. - 9. it. - 10. she.

19. 1. My name is Mary and I'm a teacher. - 2. Where did you put the books? I can't find them. - 3. My car is broken: could you lend me yours? - 4. Have you seen the movie *Titanic*? I think we will rent it. - 5. Did you talk with to Mark? I think he is looking for you. - 6. I don't like Jerry: you must quit seeing him! - 7. Can you help me with my homework? - 8. Why don't you take us to the cinema with you? - 9. Do you know where Susan is? I have to go with her to supermarket. - 10. The toys are in the garden: go and pick them up.

20. 1. this. - 2. that. - 3. this. - 4. this; that. - 5. those. - 6. this. - 7. these; those. - 8. those. - 9. this. - 10. this.

21. 1. those. - 2. these. - 3. this. - 4. these. - 5. this. - 6. this. - 7. those. - 8. that. - 9. these; that. - 10. this.

22. 1. some; any. - 2. any. - 3. any. - 4. some; some. - 5. no. - 6. any. - 7. some; any. - 8. some; some. - 9. any. - 10. no.

23. 1. anything. - 2. anything. - 3. anybody. - 4. anybody. - 5. anybody. - 6. anything. - 7. anything. - 8. anything. - 9. anybody. - 10. anything.

24. 1. something. - 2. someone; nobody. - 3. any. - 4. anything. - 5. someone. - 6. something. - 7. anything. - 8. nobody; somebody. - 9. something. - 10. something.

25. 1. Many of us love the mountains. - 2. Mary has spent several days at her sister's house. - 3. Both John and Susan like playing tennis very much. - 4. None of the two is sick. - 5. An Alice came to look for you. - 6. The defendants are both guilty. - 7. Many strange things happened in this house. - 8. Everybody is sad because of Mr Brown's death. - 9. He hasn't worked enough to get a promotion. - 10. Peter is such a good guy.

26. 1. a little. - 2. a few. - 3. few. - 4. little. - 5. a few. - 6. little. - 7. a few. - 8. a little. - 9. little. - 10. few.

27. 1. a lot of. - 2. many. - 3. a lot of; a lot of. - 4. much. - 5. a lot of. - 6. much. - 7. much. - 8. several. - 9. many. - 10. several.

28. 1. every. - 2. both. - 3. either; or - 4. both. - 5. each. - 6. neither of. - 7. every. - 8. both. - 9. either of. - 10. both.

29. 1. yours. - 2. hers. - 3. yours. - 4. mine. - 5. mine. - 6. theirs. - 7. his. - 8. its. - 9. ours. - 10. yours; mine.

30. 1. myself. - 2. yourself. - 3. ourselves. - 4. himself. - 5. themselves. - 6. herself. - 7. himself. - 8. themselves. - 9. himself. - 10. ourselves.

31. 1. They fell in love at first sight. - 2. We help each other in the times of need. - 3. Peter and Mark accused each other. - 4. The mother told her children to be good to one another. - 5. He wanted us to listen to each other.

32. 1. //. - 2. who. - 3. //. - 4. whose. - 5. whom. - 6. that. - 7. which. - 8. whose. - 9. //. - 10. whose.

33. 1. my; your. - 2. my. - 3. their. - 4. your. - 5. my. - 6. her. - 7. its. - 8. our. - 9. your. - 10. their. - 11. your. - 12. her. - 13. its. - 14. their. - 15. our.

34. 1. What do they often read? - 2. Mark always wins at tennis. - 3. The shelf is too high. - 4. This food is absolutely excellent. - 5. Fortunately the weather is good. - 6. Peter drives his car very carefully. - 7. Sometimes we go to the cinema. - 8. They did their homework easily. - 9. I go to the gym twice a week. - 10. Yesterday we almost won the lottery.

35. 1. I have always loved jazz music. - 2. Unfortunately I couldn't convince him. - 3. He changed road fast not to meet Mary. - 4. I have always done my job myself. - 5. Please, sit down in silence for few minutes and I'll explain everything to you. - 6. The sand castle we built with care fell down after ten minutes. - 7. I can't thank you enough! - 8. Jerry is on diet, but he still eats too much. - 9. Susan speaks French fluently. - 10. Alice hasn't finished her homework yet.

36. 1. I have always done what I believe in strongly. - 2. I haven't written the letter yet. - 3. Mark still loves Lucy. - 4. Do you often go to the cinema? - 5. I always say what I think. - 6. We didn't like Madonna's last album very much. - 7. Susan and John no longer live here. - 8. Have you already had lunch? - 9. Mary truly believed in what she was doing. - 10. This box isn't big enough.

37. 1. easily. - 2. loudly. - 3. slowly. - 4. hard. - 5. high.

38. 1. still. - 2. yet. - 3. someplace. - 4. tomorrow. - 5. already. - 6. behind. - 7. someday. - 8. over there. - 9. yesterday. - 10. anywhere.

39. 1. seldom. - 2. usually. - 3. ever. - 4. always. - 5. never.

40. 1. enough. - 2. almost. - 3. only. - 4. much. - 5. really.

41. 1. probably. - 2. definitely. - 3. perhaps. - 4. unfortunately. - 5. surely.

42. 1. Could you speak more slowly, please? - 2. Susan has run faster than anybody else. - 3. They have played worse than last week. - 4. Mark and Peter ran down the hill faster and faster. - 5. I can't walk as fast as you.

43. 1. on. - 2. at. - 3. on. - 4. at. - 5. in. - 6. at. - 7. on. - 8. at. - 9. in. - 10. in.

44. 1. during. - 2. since. - 3. for. - 4. for. - 5. during. - 6. for. - 7. since. - 8. during. - 9. since. - 10. for.

45. 1. in. - 2. at. - 3. in. - 4. at. - 5. at. - 6. in. - 7. at. - 8. in. - 9. at. - 10. in.

46. 1. to. - 2. from. - 3. into. - 4. to. - 5. to. - 6. to. - 7. from. - 8. into. - 9. from. - 10. to.

47. 1. Is this present for me? - 2. The cat is on the chair, not under it. - 3. «Where do you come from?». «I come from Canada». - 4. The Browns are always kind with us. - 5. We are not afraid of Jerry. - 6. I tried to go through the door but it was locked, so I went through the window of the living-room. - 7. I moved from London to Dublin. - 8. We wanted to go to the city by train but we missed it and we had to go by car. - 9. I never go to the office by bus, I always go on foot. - 10. We arrived in Cardiff at 4 p.m.

48. 1. until. - 2. by. - 3. till. - 4. by. - 5. within. - 6. by. - 7. until. - 8. by. - 9. till. - 10. by.

49. 1. across. - 2. under. - 3. through. - 4. under. - 5. across. - 6. through. - 7. under. - 8. across. - 9. over. - 10. through.

50. 1. Mary isn't afraid of dogs. - Is Mary afraid of dogs? - 2. We aren't happy. - Are we happy? - 3. He isn't hungry. - Is he hungry? - 4. They aren't bored. - Are they bored? - 5. You aren't sorry. - Aren't you sorry?

51. 1. is sad. - 2. was ill. - 3. is sleepy. - 4. are (you) mad. - 5. is cold. - 6. were happy. - 7. are (they) interested. - 8. was upset. - 9. am fine. - 10. was cheap.

52. 1. have (you) got. - 2. has got. - 3. hasn't got. - 4. haven't got. - 5. has (John) got / hasn't. - 6. have got. - 7. have you got. - 8. had got. - 9. have (Susan and John) got. - 10. haven't got.

53. 1. have a shower. - 2. had a beer. - 3. had a fight. - 4. didn't have fun. - 5. having dinner. - 6. had (an interesting) talk. - 7. have a nap. - 8. are having a picnic. - 9. have a holiday. - 10. have a quarrel.

54. 1. I had my car washed. - 2. Yesterday I had my hair cut. - 3. I can't invite you to dinner because I'm having my house painted. - 4. Has Mark had his car fixed? - 5. Do you have your windows cleaned every month? - 6. We are having a new garage built. - 7. While I was having my hair cut, police had my car taken away. - 8. Peter will have his tooth extracted. - 9. They are having their cellar cleaned. - 10. Did you have the new aerial installed?

55. 1. get up. - 2. watches. - 3. works. - 4. am. - 5. does (she) like. - 6. wants. - 7. jogs. - 8. do (you) eat. - 9. goes. - 10. speaks.

56. 1. Does Jim teach English well? - 2. Does the boy want to stay here with us? - 3. Do you study at the university? - 4. Does Mark often reply to your letters? - 5. Don't Alice go to school? - 6. Do they want to go to the sea? - 7. Don't they like swimming? - 8. Doesn't Peter like his job? - 9. Don't you see the roses over there? - 10. Do Peter and Mark play tennis every week?

57. 1. is living. - 2. is talking. - 3. are (you) writing. - 4. it is not raining. - 5. is watching. - 6. are moving out. - 7. is (Jerry) doing. - 8. are going. - 9. am reading. - 10. are (you) sitting.

58. 1. do you do; am not working. - 2. likes; is swimming. - 3. goes to; is going. - 4. is taking. - 5. don't understand; is saying. - 6. doesn't know; is doing. - 7. don't owe. - 8. are going. - 9. am bathing. - 10. is meeting; is taking. - 11. wears; watch. - 12. explodes; jumps. - 13. don't believe; always lie. - 14. wants. - 15. doesn't work.

59. 1. are playing. - 2. knows. - 3. //. - 4. //. - 5. //. - 6. //. - 7. loves. - 8. I'm playing. - 9. doesn't watch. - 10. //.

60. 1. watched. - 2. played. - 3. studied. - 4. decided. - 5. rained. - 6. lived. - 7. invited. - 8. arrived. - 9. enjoyed. - 10. died.

61. 1. bought. - 2. sent. - 3. kept. - 4. went. - 5. felt. - 6. had. - 7. drank. - 8. left. - 9. slept. - 10. saw.

62. 1. Have you ever met my sister? - 2. They haven't finished their work yet. - 3. It hasn't snowed much this year. - 4. Has Susan ever spent a holiday in the mountains? - 5. Peter has never bought a red car. - 6. Has your brother ever worked? - 7. Hasn't Robert called back? - 8. Has Alice gone to school today? - 9. I've often talked to Jim. - 10. Where have you been today?

63. 1. Did you know her father died? - 2. Did he pay his employees last week? - 3. Didn't Jim and Peter go to school together when they were kids? - 4. Did you and Susan play tennis last Saturday? - 5. Didn't she tell you to shut up? - 6. Did your parents like the new neighborhood? - 7. Didn't Robert speak to his brother yesterday? - 8. Didn't I give you back your books? - 9. When did we meet him? - 10. What did you ask me?

64. 1. went. - 2. have just met. - 3. did you see. - 4. played. - 5. have you ever travelled. - 6. haven't read. - 7. have you seen. - 8. decided. - 9. have been. - 10. have you ever been.

65. 1. After I had got up at 6 a.m. I went to the airport. After I had gone to the airport I took my flight. - 2. After Susan had gone to the post office she bought a stamp. After she had bought a stamp she sent the letter. - 3. After the cop had gone to the scene of the accident he interviewed the people involved in the accident. After he had interviewed the people involved in the accident he arrested the man who was driving. - 4. After we had made an appointment to see the new house we went to see the house. After we had seen the house we bought it. - 5. After Alice had gone to the library to take out *Sense and Sensibility* she read the book. After she had read the book she took it back to the library.

66. 1. Alice was having a shower when Peter came into the bathroom. - 2. I was watching a soccer match when Robert called. - 3. Mark and Jerry were having a coffee when they saw Jim with his girlfriend. - 4. My parents were sleeping when the burglar broke into the house. - 5. I was talking to the new boss when Liz left the office very fast. - 6. We were playing tennis when it started to rain. - 7. Mary was driving when a cat crossed the street. - 8. I was leaving the house when the phone rang. - 9. My friends were having a party when the fire started. - 10. He was skiing when he broke his leg.

67. 1. has been working. - 2. have been reading. - 3. have been watching. - 4. has been talking. - 5. has (he) been studying.

68. 1. had been working. - 2. had (you) been waiting. - 3. had (Robert) delivering. - 4. had been studying. - 5. had been walking.

69. 1. have owned. - 2. has been driving. - 3. have you been waiting. - 4. have (you) known. - 5. has been sleeping.

70. 1. I used to jog years ago. - 2. Did you use to play tennis when you where younger? - 3. We didn't use to come to this place last year. - 4. Did Mark use to be an actor when he was young? - 5. Years ago we used to live in this building.

71. 1. won't. - 2. will. - 3. will. - 4. will; will. - 5. will. - 6. won't. - 7. will. - 8. will. - 9. won't. - 10. won't.

72. 1. will be leaving. - 2. won't be watching. - 3. will be visiting. - 4. will be eating. - 5. will be wearing. - 6. will be working. - 7. will be waiting. - 8. will be fixing. - 9. will you be staying. - 10. won't be washing.

73. 1. will have finished. - 2. will have been. - 3. won't have finished. - 4. will have been spending. - 5. will have transferred. - 6. will have been working. - 7. will have saved. - 8. will have found. - 9. will have been studying. - 10. will have been teaching.

74. 1. Can he sing? Yes, he can. - 2. Can they drive? No, they can't. - 3. Can you speak French? Yes, I can. - 4. Can we ride a bike? Yes, we can. - 5. Can she dance? No, she can't. - 6. Can you play the guitar? No, I can't. - 7. Can they have a dog? Yes, they can. - 8. Can he use a computer? No, he can't. - 9. Can she play cards? No, she can't. - 10. Can we run fast? Yes, we can.

75. 1. can't. - 2. can. - 3. can. - 4. can't. - 5. can't. - 6. can't. - 7. can. - 8. can. - 9. can't. - 10. can't.

76. 1. May I have a glass of water? - 2. May I use the bathroom? - 3. May I take this seat? - 4. May I open the window? - 5. May I dance with you, Mary?

77. 1. We may not go to the cinema tonight. - 2. Susan and John may buy a new house. - 3. Lucy may not get married next year. - 4. He may help us. - 5. They may not come home late tonight.

78. 1. must respect. - 2. mustn't smoke. - 3. must study. - 4. must take. - 5. mustn't drive. - 6. must feed. - 7. must repair. - 8. mustn't talk. - 9. must go. - 10. must find.

79. 1. Shall we wear the glasses? - 2. Shall I turn on the light? - 3. Shall we go to the supermarket? - 4. Shall I turn down the volume? - 5. Shall I answer the phone?

80. 1. should. - 2. shouldn't. - 3. should. - 4. should. - 5. should. - 6. should. - 7. shouldn't. - 8. should. - 9. should. - 10. shouldn't.

81. 1. could. - 2. could. - 3. couldn't. - 4. could. - 5. could. - 6. could. - 7. couldn't. - 8. couldn't. - 9. could. - 10. couldn't.

82. 1. might. - 2. might have. - 3. might. - 4. might. - 5. might have. - 6. might. - 7. might have. - 8. might have. - 9. mightn't. - 10. mightn't.

83. 1. need. - 2. must. - 3. has to. - 4. don't have to. - 5. must. - 6. must. - 7. must. - 8. had to. - 9. needn't. - 10. must.

84. 1. may. - 2. can. - 3. can. - 4. may. - 5. might. - 6. can't. - 7. will be able. - 8. can't. - 9. may. - 10. can.

85. 1. should have. - 2. could. - 3. shouldn't. - 4. shouldn't have. - 5. shouldn't; might. - 6. couldn't. - 7. might. - 8. shouldn't. - 9. might. - 10. couldn't.

86. 1. I suddenly woke up and saw the thief. - 2. Robert got drunk and fell down. - 3. Mary left her boyfriend. - 4. We have written a long letter. - 5. I knew it was too late. - 6. Alice always forgets to take the keys. - 7. Yesterday they slept till 11 a.m. - 8. Susan said that she was very tired. - 9. I have never read a book so boring. - 10. She wore her best dress.

87. 1. fell / broke. - 2. understood. - 3. found. - 4. drove. - 5. struck. - 6. got. - 7. gone. - 8. rang. - 9. shot. - 10. bitten.

88. 1. Liz often forgets to visit me. - 2. Yesterday I read an interesting article. - 3. Last week we met our cousins. - 4. Jerry took off his coat when he entered the house. - 5. Troops were used to stop the rebellion. - 6. Robert made out that he was a student looking for a job. - 7. Liz learnt some American history in high school. - 8. Last night they came home very late. - 9. Last week I kept £ 20 for me and gave £ 10 to my friend. - 10. They have already chosen the movie to rent.

89. 1. worn. - 2. come. - 3. cooked. - 4. written. - 5. sank. - 6. meant. - 7. sold. - 8. broke; hit. - 9. had. - 10. lit.

90. 1. Have you ever been to Rome? - 2. Have they already chosen their house? - 3. Has Mark often spoken to his sister? - 4. Has he met his teacher yet? - 5. Have Liz and Peter ever hidden a secret from each other? - 6. Have you already learnt the lesson? - 7. Has Mary ever dreamt about me? - 8. Has she ever lost her patience? - 9. Have you ever sung in the shower? - 10. Have they already done their homework?

www.ingramcontent.com/pod-product-compliance
Lightning Source LLC
LaVergne TN
LVHW051351080426
835509LV00020BA/3380